GIFTS FOR KIDS THAT MONEY CAN'T BUY

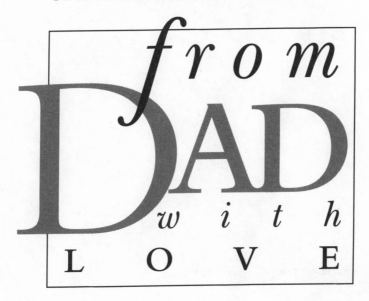

from

DAD

with

LOVE

D1531375

CHUCK AYCOCK
DAVE VEERMAN

Tyndale House Publishers, Inc.
WHEATON, ILLINOIS

The "NIV" and "New International Version" trademarks are registered in the United States
Patent and Trademark Office by International Bible Society. Use of either trademark requires
the permission of International Bible Society.

Unless otherwise noted, all Scripture quotations are taken from *The Living Bible,* copyright
© 1971 owned by assignment by KNT Charitable Trust. All rights reserved.

Scripture quotations marked (NIV) are from the *Holy Bible,* New International Version®.
Copyright © 1973, 1978, 1984 by International Bible Society. Used by permission of
Zondervan Publishing House. All rights reserved.

Library of Congress Cataloging-in-Publication Data

Aycock, Chuck.
   From dad, with love / Chuck Aycock and Dave Veerman.
     p.   cm.
   Includes bibliographical references.
   ISBN 0-8423-1333-8 :
   1. Fathers—Religious life. 2. Fatherhood (Christian theology)
I. Veerman, David. II. Title.
BV4846.A83 1994   93-39454
248.8'421—dc20

Printed in the United States of America

99 98 97 96 95 94
9   8   7   6   5   4   3   2   1

To our wives, MYRLISS AYCOCK and GAIL VEERMAN,
our closest friends and biggest cheerleaders—and they're terrific moms!

CONTENTS

PART THREE

THE GIFT OF CONFIDENCE

Chuck Aycock and Dave Veerman are veteran fathers and ministers.

Chuck and Myrllis Aycock have two sons, Craig (29) and Brian (27). Chuck worked for 33 years with Youth for Christ in Detroit; Muskegon, Michigan; and Minneapolis. He also served as an assistant to the president of YFC/USA, organizing and leading a variety of projects in the U.S. and around the world. In one of these, Harvest, Chuck led 50 American young people on a short-term missions project in South Africa. Chuck is a cofounding board member of the National Center for Fathering and currently serves as its vice president of development.

Dave and Gail Veerman are the parents of two teenage daughters, Kara (18) and Dana (15). Also a veteran of Youth for Christ (26 years in the Chicago suburbs, New Orleans, and the YFC national office), Dave left in 1988 to begin The Livingstone Corporation, a team of writers, editors, and desktop publishers. Dave has authored 25 books, including *Youth Evangelism, Reaching Kids before High School,* and *How to Apply the Bible.* He is also one of the senior editors of the *Life Application Bible.*

This book is a cooperative effort between Chuck and Dave, so the pronoun *we* is used throughout. When personal examples are given, however, the person writing is identified in parentheses, and then the pronoun *I* is used in that story.

INTRODUCTION

"Daddy's home!" My young daughters yelled their happy greeting as I (Dave) shut the car door and gathered my luggage. With outstretched arms they ran down the driveway and then embraced any part of me they could reach.

It hadn't been a long trip—just a couple of days. But the girls missed me, and it felt great to be welcomed with their love. Their next step, of course, was looking for the gifts I had brought home with me. Bubbling with excitement, Kara and Dana could hardly wait for me to open my suitcase.

When my daughters were very young, finding interesting and appropriate gifts was easy . . . and cheap. Even a plastic name tag held their interest. But as they grew older, I found myself checking out hotel and airport gift shops to find gifts they would appreciate—and I bought them, even at the inflated prices.

Good fathers enjoy giving gifts to their children. I remember Christmas mornings when my brothers, sister, and I would huddle at the top of the stairs and wait for Dad to give the signal to descend. I relive that same joy he must have felt when I watch my children anticipate and then discover their wrapped treasures every December.

I enjoy the birthday parties too. Gail and I must have miles of film and videotape of each daughter at her parties, surrounded by friends from our neighborhood and church. And we never tire of hearing clichés like "Just what I always wanted!" when each package is opened and its contents displayed.

The continual challenge for dads is to find gifts that children *want* and *need*. Adding to this dilemma, each year the size of the gift and its price increase dramatically (plastic name tags don't cut it with a teenager who wants a car!). Before long, most fathers wonder how they can continue to pay for those squeals of delight.

Well, we have good news! There are affordable gifts, and these gifts are within the reach of all fathers willing to give them. What's even better news is that our children *want* and *need* what we have to offer. Our society seems to place a dollar value on everything, so the natural question is, How much do they cost? How much money will it take to make my kids happy? But these are gifts that money *can't* buy! In addition, these presents last. When the toys have broken, the luster has worn off, and the clothes have gone out of style, these gifts remain. Best of all, unlike fads and expensive trinkets, our children really need what we fathers can give them.

All of this should come as great news in a day when many wonder whether fathers have anything at all to give to their children. Over the past several decades, the father's role has been devalued, and a dad's time spent with his family has been in steady decline. Just look at the statistics about divorce, desertion, and single mothers. According to some estimates, as many as one third of today's children will experience their parents' divorce, and close to one half will spend some time in a single-parent family before the age of 18. In the wake of the women's movement, some have even suggested that children don't really need their fathers around, except perhaps to provide financial support.

> In the past two decades, the number of children born to single parents has soared, from 12 percent of births in 1970 to more than 25 percent in 1990. Sixty percent of black children are now born to mothers without husbands.
>
> And the decline of traditional families breeds a host of problems. The National Commission on Children reports that children of a single parent are six times more likely to encounter illness and trouble in school and with the legal system.
>
> *Tom Hamburger*[1]

These days, however, we are paying for those years of decline and neglect by fathers. And many social scientists are coming to realize the vital role played by fathers.

According to Dr. Roger Thompson, coordinator of the criminal justice program at the University of Tennessee in Chatanooga, "One of the problems creating dysfunctional families is the absentee father. Statistics indicate that the increase in female-headed households is inextricably tied to the 'feminization of poverty.'"[3]

Dr. Festus Obiakor, a professor in the Department of Educational Psychology at the same university, states:

> The real issue is missing men, and the crisis in this culture is a crisis of fatherhood. You can't reach a father through legislation. You can reach his wallet in the form of child support, but you can't reach a father.
>
> We have to develop a men's movement in this country. A social movement that has little to do with politics and legislation. A movement designed to awaken renewed concern among men about their responsibility for children. To restore the pride, the rewards, the dignity, and the sense of respect that comes with caring for one's own children.
>
> *Don Eberly*[2]

Many researchers and educators have noted the role of fatherhood in enhancing self-awareness, self-knowledge, self-esteem, self-pride, self-responsibility, and self-production in children. . . . A good father should be the pillar of his household. He should be the provider, as much as possible. . . . It is no wonder that divorce disrupts the equilibrium of children, especially when the father leaves the home and refuses to pay his child support.[4]

The effects of absent fathers on children is spelled out by Samuel Osherson in *Finding Our Fathers:* "If father is not there to provide a confident, rich model of manhood, then the boy is left in a vulnerable position." The author further explains this point:

My father is the most important person in my life. He is not only a loving father to me, but a good example and my best friend. There are not too many teenagers who can say that their father is their best friend. He told me that his main goal in life was to raise his children to the best of his ability.

I found out at an early age that I needed to have a personal relationship with God. Not to know all the facts about him, but to know him personally. My father wants me to know how much God loves and accepts me. Therefore, I feel that I don't need to perform for my acceptance.

All my friends really like my dad and say he is so cool. My dad is a very wise man. He is always there to listen and give advice to me when I need it, which is usually every day.

Dad's confidence in me makes me never doubt the possibilities of what I can accomplish. I thank God every day for giving me such a loving father.

Thanks, Dad.

David, junior in high school

When a person is absent, either physically or psychologically, you need to explain why that person is not there. Father absence provides fertile ground for a son's mistaken imaginings about his father. The son's understanding of his father's absence is crucial. That is where sons start to idealize or degrade their fathers, misidentifying with them, and struggling with shame and guilt themselves.[5]

In addition to those important responsibilities shared by all fathers, the Christian father is vital in bringing children to Christ. Children need their fathers. In prophesying the role that John the Baptist would play in preparing the way for Jesus, Malachi wrote, "He will turn the hearts of the fathers to their children, and the hearts of the children to their fathers" (Malachi 4:6, NIV).

Your children need you. Your presence is a gift that *only* you can give!

There are other gifts that we fathers can give to our sons and daughters. We can't buy these gifts at the airport or any other store, and yet we have them. They are already ours to give. But these gifts aren't cheap—they cost in time, effort, and concentration.

This book will help you discover these gifts that you can give to your children. They are the most important gifts your children will ever receive. Isn't it great we can give gifts that money can't buy!

From Dad, with love.

Dad Who?

Who knows of a special dad?
A dad who brings confidence to his son
And beauty to his daughter.
Where on earth is he, please come.

I sat and pondered of what makes a father
And I found it easy to know
For I have been in the presence
Of a father who helped me to grow.

Who is this man you may ask?
He is my own father I stand and shout.
I have known him for many years
There is no one like him without a doubt.

A father must be committed
To his God and his family.
This is a very difficult task
But he has no choice you see.

A father must be available
To his wife and his kids.
Nothing is more important in life
Than to do what God bids.

A father must love
His Father and his responsibility.
What a small sacrifice to love
Such gifts God has given, please believe.

A father must be involved
Not only in time but in quality.
Where else should he be
Than present with his beloved family.

A father must be so many things at once
Where does he find the strength?
He must go to the Almighty
Or he will find himself on the brink.

A father will fail, yes this is true.
But how he goes about failing
That is where his heart comes through.
For in the end will he be standing?

Yes, I know of a father like this,
He is my own, I call him by name.
How blessed I am to have his blood
One day to be like him, one in the same.

Brian Aycock
5 October 1992.

PART ONE

THE *gift* OF PROTECTION

Virtually all living creatures protect their young. Without protection, innocent and vulnerable little ones would be defenseless against the elements and a variety of predators.

Good parents will make every effort to keep their children from harm—from placing poisons out of reach to insisting on seat belts and biking helmets, from teaching them about "stranger danger" to teaching them to look both ways before crossing the street. That's physical protection. It involves removing threats to safety, putting a roof over the family, and teaching children to be careful and aware. And it's important.

But children need more than physical protection—that's just the beginning. Children also need to know that, whatever happens in life, there is a place—a physical location—that will shut out fears, the attacks of those who don't like them, and anyone else who would threaten their emotional or spiritual well-being. Children need an environment that has all the protection they require: a place called home.

Money can't buy this gift of protection, but you as a father can provide it.

CHAPTER 1

Provide Comfort

WHEN Myrllis and I (Chuck) brought Craig, our first son, home from the hospital as a newborn baby, we knew he was dependent on us for his very life. He was helpless. He needed protection from harm, and he couldn't provide for his own physical needs. Although our lives were disrupted by this new arrival, we were willing to make any sacrifice necessary: a sturdy crib, the right food, cute clothes, and weird feeding times. Craig was also dependent on us for his emotional well-being. He needed a safe, comfortable environment in which to grow up and become the person God created him to be.

Homes need to be safe, protective environments for children, places where no one from the outside can harm them. To provide that kind of comfort means giving our children a sense of home, a sense of heritage, and a sense of warmth.

A SENSE OF HOME

Providing comfort for children begins by giving them positive feelings about home.

What comes to mind when you hear the word *home?* What memories ease their way into your consciousness? Think of the familiar smells and sounds and feelings that filled your early years.

For many, those memories are precious—the scent of homemade bread, hot out of the oven, waiting to be sliced and buttered; the screen door slamming behind as you enter the kitchen for some cold lemonade on a hot summer day; dark corners in the basement and attic where you and your friends played hide-and-seek; the squeaky chair in the living room; relatives jamming the house for a Thanksgiving feast and the delicious smell of turkey and trimmings as they are being carried into the dining room; the heavy quilt pulled over your head to warm you during cold winter nights; games and laughs and squeals of delight. Positive, wonderful memories.

For others, however, the word *home* conjures only painful thoughts: deprivation, loneliness, even abuse.

Every child needs good memories of home—positive feelings of the house or apartment where they were wanted and accepted—a safe place. Home should be where family members can come to regroup, to renew their spirits. Children should know that they will be missed if they are not there. Home should be as comfortable as an old shoe—it just feels right.

Fathers can provide a sense of home by offering children an environment where they can be themselves without having to be perfect and fit into the perfect family.

Ed was almost obsessed with being a good father because he had never known his own father, who had deserted the family when Ed was a baby. Ed felt that his house had to be just right—wallpaper, furniture, toys, everything—nothing was too good for his kids. Unfortunately, the kids could never be too good for Ed. Because of his subconscious need to succeed at parenting, Ed pushed his two sons and one daughter to be excellent in everything they did, from Little League baseball to attendance at Sunday school. There was little room for imperfection. The children were expected to clean their rooms, practice the piano, and do assigned chores around the house without a hint of whining or complaining. For Ed's children, home became a tense place where they couldn't relax, act their age, or be themselves.

This doesn't mean that our homes should be run by children, with no discipline, responsibilities, or obedience. But there should be an attitude of acceptance and an atmosphere of give-and-take. Imagine if Ed came home from work and, instead of checking to see if the kids had completed their chores and were doing their homework, threw his coat on the couch, took off his tie and shoes, and surprised each one with a hug or tickling or wrestling. What a difference that would make! And what if at the dinner table, Ed honestly admitted that he had been wrong in a discussion earlier in the day with Mom and his little girl? You can almost see her eyes opened wide in amazement. Those actions may seem small, but for Ed they would be significant, removing tension and making home a fun place where real people live.

What can you do to give your children a sense of home?

> Barry Shell. That name may not mean anything to you, but to me, it's the name of my super dad. Being deaf since infancy, he's taught me sign language and not to give up. He also taught me that you should be happy and satisfied with what God gave you and not to take your anger out on other people.
>
> He doesn't only teach me, I teach him too. Sometimes I help him on his speech and language skills. He is also a strong and proud father. Sometimes when I

practice the piano, he'll come and sit down in the re-
cliner next to the piano and put his hand on it to feel
the vibrations. That makes me proud that I have a
father who is happy with who I am and the things I
do. Sometimes I wish he could hear—actually, almost
all the time. I wish we could do things a hearing father
and daughter could do.

I guess all I'm trying to say is that it didn't matter
and still doesn't matter what he taught or is going to
teach me. He accepts me just like I am, and I accept
him as my dad.

It still seems like whatever he teaches is easy to understand and hard to forget.

Andrea, sixth grade

A SENSE OF HERITAGE

Another key ingredient for providing comfort is to give
children a sense of heritage. This means helping them understand their place in the family and their link to the past and to
the future.

Giving a sense of heritage involves building positive memories of family. What good memories do you have of growing
up? Think of the fun activities you did with your dad or mom,
such as shopping for groceries every Friday night followed by
a visit to Dairy Queen. Or maybe you can recall vacations
planned by the whole family. Think of how you celebrated
birthdays and other special events.

Family Memories

A sense of heritage can also include a close look at the
relatives, helping children understand their link to the family's past. This can begin with explaining what is special
about your surname and their mother's maiden name. See

how far back you can trace your family roots on both sides. And talk about your ethnic, cultural, and national heritage. This is where it's great to get the grandparents involved. Let them reminisce—children love to hear stories about when Dad or Mom was their age. By the way, those stories will also help keep you humble when you are reminded of your teenage pranks and the times you got in trouble. And be sure to discuss their spiritual heritage—explain when you accepted Christ as Savior and how you have depended on him over the years.

Spend time remembering as a family. Talk about places you've lived—neighborhoods, schools, churches. If possible, take the family on a tour of the neighborhood where you grew up. Show the kids your old house with the front porch where you played with your brother, the playground where you fell off the swing, the elementary school where you were a crossing guard and the teacher's pet, the junior high where your voice changed and you fell in love for the first time, the high school where you had the solo in the musical and almost got suspended for the practical joke that backfired, the stadium where you played football and ran track. If you can't go back physically, at least get out the pictures, letter jacket, awards, and yearbooks. All of this will help your children see you as a real person; they will be able to put you in context. They will also see a lot of themselves in you.

Family Traditions

I (Chuck) can remember the long trips to Grandpa and Grandma's house and the special times I spent with my grandfather, breaking open a watermelon and eating it right there in the field. What made it even sweeter was that it was a secret just between the two of us.

One family tradition that stands out in my (Dave's) mind is

7

our annual caroling visits on Christmas Eve. After a special meal, Mom and Dad would gather all five kids into our station wagon and make the rounds in the community, singing carols for our pastor, close friends, and relatives. At each stop, we would be warmly welcomed and treated to Christmas cookies or fudge. When we finally returned home, each child would be allowed to open one Christmas present. Then we would be hustled off to bed, where we would try to fall asleep so that morning would come quickly.

Family traditions help children feel connected. Being able to say "We do this every year" is all part of being in the family. What traditions can you begin? Use your imagination. You might begin by celebrating the holidays in a special way: reading the Christmas story by candlelight, yelling "Happy New Year!" at the stroke of midnight, creating handmade valentines, getting up at the crack of dawn for an Easter sunrise breakfast, putting the flag out on Independence Day with great ceremony, carving weird faces on pumpkins before Halloween, or making a family "Thanksgiving list."

Many families develop traditions around food, especially those unique, ethnic dishes. Or it may just be Dad's special chili, pizza on Friday nights, or popcorn with table games.

Other traditions can be developed around birthday celebra-

Each year at Christmastime we have a "candle-lighting ceremony." Everyone sits in a circle and holds an unlighted candle. One at a time, we share something from the previous year we're thankful to God for and something we're hoping for in the new year. After one individual has shared, he or she lights the next person's candle, and it continues until all the candles are lighted.

This has always been one of my favorite traditions, representing the unity of our family and dependence upon the Lord. It gives all of us a sense of spiritual renewal and optimism for the coming year. My mother originated this ceremony, and it will certainly be passed down to the generations to come.

Danae Dobson[1]

tions, the last day of summer vacation, the time to plant bulbs in the fall, large piles of raked leaves, the first snowfall, the first robin, and so forth. Any occasion can be a reason for starting a tradition. And it's great when Dad takes the lead in beginning and leading these traditions.

Family Projects

Another way to give children a sense of heritage is to get everyone involved in a family project. These projects help in two ways: first, they focus on family, and second, they bring the family together when they're being done.

This is another opportunity for imagination and creativity. These projects should be exciting and fun for everyone. You could write a family motto or design a family crest to be displayed in the foyer or family room. You could gather all those photos collected from the birthdays and vacations over the years and make a family album . . . or two . . . or three! You could review your old movies and videotapes and label them correctly. Families with a bit more ambition and patience could research and draw a family tree. You might even want to plan a family reunion.

As mentioned earlier, I (Dave) grew up in a family of five children. Although we are now scattered all over the country and our parents have died, every two years we get together for a family reunion. My daughters really enjoy seeing their aunts, uncles, and cousins. In fact, they want to make sure we continue this tradition even after they've left home.

Some fathers compile a "life

The average five-year-old, we are told, spends 25 *minutes* a week in close interaction with his father and 25 *hours* a week in close interaction with the TV. No wonder that in a recent survey of kindergartners and their priorities, Dad finished second to the boob tube.

The moral of the story? If we're not committed to our children, we can't expect them to be committed to us.

Greg Johnson and Mike Yorkey[2]

notebook" for each child, beginning with the child's sixth birthday. The notebook could be a scrapbook, a photo album, a three-ring binder—whatever works for the father and child. The notebook belongs to the son or daughter, who keeps it in a place of his or her choosing. At the front of the notebook, Dad writes a paragraph about that child's importance to him. This is followed by a record of the daughter or son's accomplishments and special events. The notebook contains ribbons, certificates, newspaper clippings, and pictures of family and friends—as many as they want to include. These fathers are sure to feature events such as the first Easter dress, the first fish caught, the first bike, the first time on snow skis, and records of other momentous occasions. The notebook also includes the four life concepts (explained in chapter 7). A life notebook can be a powerful way to build self-esteem and help a child feel included. Family projects can draw the family close, helping children feel that they belong.

Family Activities

In addition to special projects, fathers can organize and lead family activities. I (Dave) like to take my girls to community athletic events, such as high school and college football games. But I also recognize that my teenagers enjoy going to the mall; so every now and then we go there as a family. Another activity that we have enjoyed over the past few years is to attend a musical in downtown Chicago. It's a special night on the town for the four of us. So far we've seen *Phantom of the Opera* and *Les Miserables.* Although it's expensive, I know I can afford it when I hear the rave reviews from Kara and Dana.

Activities don't have to be limited to entertainment; they can include work as well. How about raking leaves in the fall or cleaning up in the spring? Or you might want to have an annual garage sale.

These activities, like the traditions and projects, help to build positive memories. Even if the events are small, you are doing something as a family. Healthy families do a lot of activities together. They work together, play together, go places together, and eat together.

Family Councils

Simply stated, family councils are regular times for sitting down and talking about family life. These meetings may involve discussing rules and chores, making decisions, and solving problems. But mostly they include sharing, affirming, and praying. These are times for the family to check in with each other, to see how everyone is doing. During these meetings, Dad and Mom need to share their struggles and ask for advice, help, and prayer. Family councils will be covered in detail in chapter 2.

Like the race cars and the orchestra, a family needs someone to set the pace and the tempo. When the pace has been properly fixed, the pacecar gets out of the way; so does an effective father. When the tempo has been set and the soloist steps into the spotlight, the conductor gives him opportunity to perform; so does the father. Without the pacecar or the conductor, you have confusion. Without an effective father, a family struggles.
Gordon MacDonald[3]

Here's what happened when I (Chuck) didn't let my son see what I was thinking and feeling when I was going through some tough times. He told me: "Dad, I wish you would have let me see you struggle with spiritual issues. Then it would have been all right for me to admit that I wasn't doing well in my spiritual growth. I really believed that there was something wrong with me and my relationship to God." That was difficult to accept, but my son was right. I grew up believing that if I looked good and didn't have many problems, my boy would want to be like me.

Wrong. Instead, he thought that *he* was the problem. This was another big lesson Dad learned!

"Whoa!" you say. "I didn't bargain for that much involvement with my kids. Who has the time?"

That's an understandable reaction, but if your children are to grow up to be healthy adults, it will take your time. And that's a gift that only you can give. This means an investment of time with each child, individually.

Spending time on family traditions, family activities, family projects, family memories, and family councils is an investment that will reap tremendous dividends. It provides a foundation for really getting to know children and their heroes, friends, hurts, and fears. We also learn how they are processing life and their hopes and dreams. And they get to see us as fellow strugglers with life's hurt, pain, and disappointments.

You may not have thought of any of these ideas before. That's OK. Or your dad might not have been a good model to follow. Don't be discouraged. Being a father is a process, not an event. It's never too late to start this process, regardless of where you are with your family.

A SENSE OF WARMTH

We also make home a place of comfort for our children by giving them a sense of warmth. Do you remember coming in from shoveling the driveway on a blustery winter day and being greeted with a hug, a blanket, and a mug of hot chocolate that made you feel warm, loved, and comfortable all over?

Our kids need that kind of feeling too. A warm place for children is a home where they are accepted for who they are without having to prove anything; a place where they can share their struggles about the outside world without fear of being betrayed or hurt.

Years ago Myrllis and I (Chuck) had just moved to a city on

Lake Michigan. Our new home was yet to be completed and we couldn't delay our arrival date; but friends allowed us to stay in a beautiful cabin right on Lake Michigan with a stunning view. By mid-September most of the summer homes were empty. An early fall storm was beginning to build, so the wind was howling and the waves were pounding. I was home early, alone, when suddenly my six-year-old burst through the front door with a look of terror on his face. Before I could get a word out, he blurted: "I knew Mom was gone, and so I would be here by myself, and this place makes weird sounds when the wind blows hard." By this time his look had changed to one of relief, and he continued. "Dad, am I glad you're here! I love you." The empty house, cold and scary, was changed to a place of warmth and security simply because I was there.

Home

Golden rooms to call your own,
  a cozy atmosphere
The welcome glow with warmth
    inside,
  with loved ones ever near
A home is where you keep your
    heart,
  where peace and joy abound
A place where you can be your-
    self
  and the love of God is found
Home is a restful haven
  filled with joy and tenderness
A place you never want to leave
  for home means happiness.
    Emily Schaffer,
    Plymouth, Minnesota

Fathers can set the warmth level by being real and showing their loving and caring side, and by honestly sharing their struggles and mistakes. In the past, fathers thought they had to wear a strong facade—to be the answer man who never had problems. Those dads had to look strong even if they didn't feel that way.

We fathers have a way of not saying the words we want to say and should say. We don't let our families see our emotions. We are so proud of our children and their mother, but we often can't (or don't know how to) express what's in our heart. It's as though we assume our children should know how we feel. Maybe that's because our fathers rarely told us how they felt. What we wanted above all else was to please our fathers. Funny—that's not what we want from our kids; all we want is for them to be happy and secure. But we are stingy with our praise as though it were all in a single basket and had to last a lifetime. Or maybe we worry that intimacy will betray our vulnerability.

Having a home with comfort and warmth doesn't mean it's free of pain and disappointments. Instead, it's the place where family members can admit to having had a bad day, where Mom and Dad can admit to having had an argument. Members of a healthy family know that life isn't easy and that it's difficult to live together in harmony. But they are committed to each other, learning together through the crises of life.

> My dad works too much. I don't know what he does, but it must be bad because he's never home. Two months ago, maybe three, I don't remember, he had to stay home from work for two whole weeks. It was fun. I didn't want to go to school because when my dad is home, I want to be there. He does lots of things, tells me stories, wrestles with me, listens to what I have learned in school. But best of all, when he's there, it is like summer time all the time because summer is when we go on vacation and we do lots of fun things.
>
> I wish my dad would get laid off again so it would be like summer every day when I get home. And he would have time to talk to me everyday, not just work.
>
> Jodey, second grade

Jodey can't have all her wishes. But couldn't she have a home where she could feel the warmth of summer from her dad because he spent time with her and listened to her concerns? And shouldn't your kids have a place like that too?

Bring warmth to your home. Give your children the gift of protection by making your home a comfortable place, with a sense of home, a sense of heritage, and a sense of warmth.

HOME: A PLACE WHERE THEY CELEBRATE YOU JUST BEING THERE.

THINK IT THROUGH

1. What comes to your mind when you hear the word *home?*

2. What room of the home you grew up in gives you the warmest memories?

3. What were your favorite family traditions?

4. What traditions are you establishing (or would you like to establish) in your family today?

5. What activities would you like to introduce to your family?

6. What can you do to give your children a sense of heritage?

Check out these related Bible passages:
Exodus 3:15; 13:14; Deuteronomy 32:7; Joshua 4:4-7; 24:15; Hebrews 12:1-2.

CHAPTER 2

Set Boundaries

IMAGINE a football game with no boundaries. The offensive and defensive teams take the field. The linemen arrange themselves in a haphazard pattern, but at the snap of the ball no flag is thrown for offsides because there are no yard markers and no line of scrimmage. The quarterback completes a pass to a wide receiver, who runs off the field, into the stands, down the stairs, around the Gatorade table, and back onto the field. No referees signal out-of-bounds because there are no sideline markers. The defense isn't worried at this turn of events, however, because there is also no goal line. Chaos and confusion would reign, with players unsure of what to do and questioning even the object of the game.

Boundaries are important. A river without boundaries becomes a flood, causing great damage. A life without boundaries becomes a moral and emotional morass.

Yet we live in a world where all the boundaries are being pushed back or removed, a world with no holds barred. If you want it, buy it! If you have a craving, satisfy it! If it feels good, do it! Whether it's the lack of morality in our sexual relationships or truthfulness in the workplace, there seem to be few guidelines left to govern our lives.

Our culture seems to want nothing that would limit individualistic freedom of enjoyment. But this sky-is-the-limit attitude has had a disastrous effect on every area of our lives, resulting in alcohol and drug abuse, sexually transmitted diseases, AIDS, child abuse, and other painful social problems. If there are no limits, no out-of-bounds markers, then children believe they can do anything and go anywhere. But as in our hypothetical football game, the result is chaos and meaninglessness.

> The divorce rate remains, stubbornly, one out of two. The out-of-wedlock birthrate has tripled since 1970; it is among the highest in the "developed" world. A nauseating buffet of dysfunctions has attended these trends—an explosion in child abuse, crime, learning disabilities, welfare dependency, name your pathology.
>
> *Joe Klein*[1]

Many fathers are confused about their role in setting boundaries for the family. This is especially upsetting to fathers in the U.S. because, during the last decade, parents have provided the greatest wealth for their families in American history. Fathers are thinking, and saying, "What else can I do? I've given my kids everything they need, haven't I?"

Our children need more than money and material possessions. In fact, as the wealth of the American family has increased, crime and abuse have also increased. Economic indicators cannot measure the values held by children or the suffering felt by broken families. Remember, the GNP (gross national product) also includes the money spent building prisons to house a lost generation. The cost of replacing the gift of time spent with Dad for store-bought gifts is measured in drug counseling in elementary schools, suicide hotlines, teen-pregnancy centers, and clinics for battered children.

Several years ago, a commission of educational, political, medical, and business leaders met to examine the problems of American children. Entitled "Code Blue," the report concluded that "never before has one generation of American teenagers been less healthy, less cared for, or less prepared for life than their parents were at the same age."[3]

The question for us fathers is, Did our providing materially for our children give them a greater security and boundaries for their identity to grow and flourish? The answer: No!

> O**ur wealth has been accompanied by an equally spectacular rise in all forms of crime, family abandonment, child neglect, suicide, widespread adoption of destructive behavior and an exponential growth of drug and alcohol abuse.**
>
> *Roger Freeman*[2]

- Suicide has increased 300 percent since 1950 and is now the second leading cause of death among adolescents.
- Teen pregnancy has risen 621 percent since 1940. More than a million teenage girls get pregnant each year. Over 85 percent of teenage boys who impregnate teenage girls eventually abandon them.
- Every year substance abuse claims younger victims with harder drugs. The average age for first-time drug use is now 13 years old.[4]

The Code Blue report made an important point: The most basic cause of suffering is profoundly self-destructive behavior—drinking, drugs, violence, and promiscuity. It's a crisis of behavior and belief: a crisis of character!

This problem will not be solved with money, clinics, or medicine because its roots go deep into the hearts and souls of children. It impacts all of our families and is deeply disturbing because it leaves a legacy of broken lives.

Part of the answer is setting boundaries for our children, giving moral guidelines and rules for living that will protect them and equip them to live in a disconnected and disturbed society.

A world without boundaries is unkind and unhealthy. A family without boundaries is sad and insecure.

There are two types of boundaries: negative and positive. Negative boundaries are rules and regulations that show a child how *not* to act. They tell when a child is out-of-bounds, off-limits, in danger, wrong, or disobedient. Positive boundaries are guidelines and goals that tell a child what to do, how to act, and how to live.

RULES AND REGULATIONS

These boundaries sound threatening and restrictive. Perhaps that's why parents, especially fathers, find them so difficult to set and enforce. We don't like to say no to our children—especially when they're very young—and make them cry, whine, or pout. It's more enjoyable to indulge their wishes with candy and other gifts and then watch their faces light up with joy and gratitude. But family rules and regulations are important gifts that demonstrate love for our kids.

I (Dave) remember my first camp as a full-time Campus Life staff member. I wanted to be liked by the students and to build close relationships with them, so I found it difficult to be a policeman and rule enforcer. As the executive director announced the camp rules on the first night, I thought, *Boy, that's a job I wouldn't like. I'm glad he's the bad guy and not me.* But I soon observed how the rules kept the campers safe and working together. Just a few years later, after seeing firsthand the importance of the rules, I volunteered to make that dreaded camp speech.

Think of the rules for your children as a wall that provides limits and *protection*. The wall shows children how far they can go and gives them a feeling of security.

Establishing the limits should begin with you and your wife discussing this whole topic thoroughly. Talk through rules in general areas such as mealtimes, school and homework, friends, church, household responsibilities, language, property, relationships with family members, and so forth. Make these regular discussions, changing and adapting rules as the children grow and mature.

The next step is to explain each rule to your children. If they are very young, you will have to begin with a simple explanation of the rule and the punishment for breaking it. Often, of course, the explanation won't need to be given until the need arises (parents can't anticipate *every* potential bad behavior). For example, if your young son repeats a swearword that he has heard on the playground, you should take him aside and talk with him about it immediately. Explain why the word is unacceptable and that you don't want him to use it. Outline the punishment he will receive if he uses the word in the future. Follow the same procedure for fighting with a brother or sister, forgetting to make his bed, or causing a disturbance in Sunday school.

> Much has been written about the dangers of harsh, oppressive, unloving discipline; these warnings are valid and should be heeded. However, the consequences of oppressive discipline have been cited as justification for the abdication of leadership. That is foolish. There are times when a strong-willed child will clench his little fists and dare his parents to accept his challenges. He is not motivated by frustrations or inner hostility, as it is often supposed. He merely wants to know where the boundaries lie and who's available to enforce them.
>
> *James Dobson*[5]

Be sure to make a distinction between careless acts (children acting their age) and defiant or disobedient behavior. The latter are much more serious and should be dealt with accordingly. These could involve everything from a child in a high chair who refuses to eat her peas and throws them at you while saying "No!" to an adolescent who tries to cover up a curfew violation. The defiant attitude is the problem more than the act.

When enforcing a rule, and especially when punishing a child for breaking a rule, act seriously, calmly, and lovingly. If you scream, yell, and otherwise lose your cool, the focus suddenly turns to your behavior and off of what the child has done. And the conflict will escalate rapidly. Don't let a screaming match result from a simple act of disobedience.

In my work with junior-high students, I (Dave) continually have to enforce rules. Because of the dramatic physical, mental, and emotional changes in adolescents, they find it difficult to sit still, keep their hands to themselves, and be quiet. I have found that kids respect my authority, and they think no less of me because I insist on their compliance. But I must treat them with respect. If I look Ted in the eye, put a hand on his shoulder, and say firmly, "Ted, that is not acceptable. The next time it happens I will have to move you to the other side of the room," Ted listens and cooperates. If, on the other hand, I were to yell at Ted and embarrass him in front of everyone in the youth group, Ted would decide immediately that I am a jerk and turn me off. Going ballistic only makes a bad situation worse.

Punishment provides an important step in setting boundaries. Children need to learn that actions have consequences. And when you consistently follow through and administer the punishment you promised for the misdeed, you build your credibility. You also build a sense of security in the child: he or she knows what to expect from you and thus how to act and how to respond to you.

Punishments should vary according to the severity of the infraction and the age of the child. The guiding principle, however, should always be "Let the punishment fit the crime." Perhaps the most effective punishment for children of any age is removing privileges or restricting freedom. Sitting a child in a corner for a half hour to think things over, sending a child to bed early without dessert, curtailing TV viewing for a while, adding jobs to the child's household chores, and keeping the child indoors, helping you, instead of playing with friends can all be very effective for making your point. The teenage version of this is "grounding." Be creative, but be firm and follow through.

You may want to discuss the punishment with your child, allowing him or her to choose among a few options. I (Dave) found it helpful to ask Kara or Dana what she would do in my situation if she were the parent. At times, of course, they said they would let the child do whatever she wanted; but usually they would try to see the situation from my point of view even though they didn't like what they saw. An excellent resource on this subject is *The New Dare To Discipline* by Dr. James Dobson (Tyndale House Publishers, 1992).

> When properly applied, loving discipline works! It stimulates tender affection, made possible by *mutual* respect between a parent and a child. It bridges the gap which otherwise separates family members who should love and trust each other. It allows the God of our ancestors to be introduced to our beloved children. It permits teachers to do the kind of job in classrooms for which they are commissioned. It encourages a child to respect other people and live as a responsible, constructive citizen.
>
> *James Dobson*[6]

Both parents should be involved in setting and enforcing the family rules—Mom and Dad need to work together, communicate, and support each other. But the father's role is critical. You need to be involved and not abdicate leadership in the home. And neither parent should paint the other as the dreaded enforcer: "Wait till your father/mother gets home!" You're in it together.

Rules and regulations provide a feeling of safety and security for children.

GUIDELINES AND GOALS

Family rules and regulations are the protective walls, telling kids what they may not or should not do. Guidelines and goals, on the other hand, point children in the right direction and tell them what they may and should do.

As with rules and regulations, deciding on guidelines and goals for children and the whole family should begin with Mom and Dad thinking, discussing, and deciding together. Again, this will not involve just one meeting where everything is discussed and decided for the lifetime of each child; it will be an ongoing process, with many midcourse corrections.

Every parent dreams of what the precious newborn will become. We begin with great ideals and hopes for our children. Then we soon get so overwhelmed with daily parenting tasks that we forget to help them set goals and achieve their dreams. But these positive boundaries are just as important as the negative ones. We don't want our kids just to avoid doing what is wrong and bad; we want them to do what is right and good also. Don't

> Some fathers demand obedience but fail to establish a loving relationship. As the child becomes older and moves into his teen years, no bond or closeness has ever been established. I've heard fathers declare with incredulity, "But John always obeyed me. I can't understand why he's suddenly so rebellious." Unfortunately, the father was unable to understand the rebellion because through the years, he had never made the effort to understand his son.
>
> *Clyde M. Narramore*[7]

just assume the role of family policeman and judge. Also act as guidance counselor, investment broker, and tour guide.

Begin by writing out your dream for your child. What kind of person do you want him or her to become? One father wrote:

> I want Sarah to be a solid Christian, committed to Jesus Christ and putting her faith into practice in her life. If she marries, her husband should also have Christ as Lord of his life so that together they will establish a solid, Christian home. I also want Sarah to be
>
> - well educated—thinking and thoughtful
> - a good citizen
> - compassionate for the needs of others
> - trained for a career but willing to be a full-time, stay-at-home mom
> - a wonderful wife and mother

As you can see, the list could go on and on, but it's important to discuss these dreams and put them in writing. This will enable you to take the next step of thinking about how your child will achieve those goals.

What could Sarah's mom and dad do, for example, to help her become "a solid Christian, committed to Jesus Christ and putting her faith into practice in her life"? I'm sure you can think of all sorts of possibilities, including being a good role model for Sarah and involving her in church activities.

To help in this process, set five kinds of goals: spiritual, physical, intellectual, emotional, and social. Decide on the goals for each area. Then think of courses of action and specific activities that will help move your child in the right direction. Again, your decisions will be affected greatly by the age of each child and her natural gifts and abilities. But you should be able to outline a multitude of guidelines and activities, including music lessons, little league sports, study habits, social events, family devotions, eating and sleeping habits, family vacations, Sunday school, summer camp, and so forth.

Intellectual boundaries include time set aside for homework, the consequences of good or bad grades, choosing courses in high school, and so forth.

Social boundaries should include allowance—how much and at what age? Think of when you will allow your kids to begin working for money and how much time they can work as they get older. If they can go into debt, how much and for what?

Social boundaries also include friends: how old do they have to be to be able to sleep over with a friend? Think of how you will handle the wrong friends, and at what age you will allow your son or daughter to single date. Many of these guidelines need to be agreed upon before puberty. A good rule of thumb is to stay two years ahead of your children from fourth grade through eighth grade and three years from ninth grade on. Bob, whose oldest daughters are 16 and 14, explained that the main reason for his teenagers feeling good about their boundaries is that he came to an understanding and agreement with them before they were 12.

Social guidelines should also include how to respond to authority: parents, teachers, coaches, pastors, police officers, and others.

Although your children won't jump for joy and enthusiastically participate in every activity you prescribe or willingly follow every guideline you present, they will appreciate your concern. Even when kids resist, they gain a sense of security from your boundaries and know that you care.

In this whole process of establishing and enforcing boundaries, it is important to offer positive reinforcement—rewards for compliance and achievement—not just punishment for disobedience or falling short. When your daughter works hard in school and does her best, regardless of the grades, reward her with a special meal or surprise gift. When your son runs hard and finishes the race, give him a hug and take him out for ice cream on the way home. When the Sunday school teacher tells you about your child's positive contribution to the class, make a point of praising your child for his behavior. And one more reason for positively reinforcing your children at home is that most of the stimulation they receive *outside* the home is negative.

FAMILY COUNCIL

Many families have been reviving an old strategy for developing family unity. This strategy works; in fact, if used once a week, it can reduce significantly the probability of a child having serious problems with delinquency, alcohol, and drugs.

The strategy is a "family council" or "family meeting"—a gathering of all family members at a specific place and time to talk things over. In some families, the organization is loose, with ideas and thoughts shared spontaneously. In others, the family council functions more formally, like a board of directors. In either case, the meetings help define family life and focus on individual, personal involvement in family activities.

The basic structure would involve cochairpersons (mother and father) and other members (children). A single-parent family would have just one chairperson. For the meetings to be effective, at least one child should be at least six years old.

The regular meetings could be held on a weekday evening after dinner, early Saturday morning, or on Sunday afternoon—whatever is best for the family. But special meetings may be called by any family member. As an incentive and to add fun, serve refreshments at the conclusion of each regular meeting.

Most business can be handled in 15 minutes; after 30 minutes, effectiveness and efficiency drop dramatically. The agenda for each meeting should include items such as work schedules, school events, family assignments, needed rides, homework deadlines, music or talent lessons, significant milestones and achievements, important decisions, etc. The meetings should also be where conflicts are resolved and goals are set. Family council meetings provide

- a sense of belonging to each family member (if the person is not present, he or she will be missed)
- opportunities to show a caring attitude for each family member's activities
- a sense of security
- essential information for emergencies
- a sense of unity—especially when making decisions together

The meetings also eliminate many last-minute surprises: "Oh, I need seven dozen cookies by 8:00 A.M. tomorrow!"

Children who live in a predictable environment begin to feel that they have some control over their world, and therefore begin to develop confidence in themselves and their abilities. Knowing what the negative consequences of a particular behavior will be increases their sense of satisfaction when they are able to avoid those consequences.

Pat Gardner,
from Mary Ann Little
and Kevin Karlson[8]

To remind family members of the meetings and to help them prepare, write the date of the next meeting and specific agenda items on a sheet of paper and post it in the kitchen. Allow kids to add to the agenda any items that they first clear with one of the cochairpersons.

To provide a change of pace for some of our family council meetings, we (Chuck and Myrllis) would bring unique projects to the table, such as placemats that had games, riddles, or interesting questions on them. We would rotate the leadership from meeting to meeting so that everyone had a chance to be chairperson. At times our boys would vote to extend the length of the meeting because they were enjoying the discussion (or they were about to win a game).

Actually, providing a sense of boundaries in life is the true aim of discipline, a word with the same Latin root as "disciple." Originally, *discipline* did not mean punishing unruly children, but teaching, guiding, and instilling inner controls.

Here's what a 32-year-old inmate wrote about his absent father and the impact on his life:

> To my father,
>
> Where have you been all my life? Why weren't you ever around when I needed you? I wish I knew you more better than as a friend! You never taught me any good things! Things I needed to know about life. I wish that someday you will finally quit bs-ing around and talk to me like a real father and son relationships should. There are so many things we need to say to each other, things that haven't been said or done. Why did you leave us at such a young age? We had so many problems that we couldn't solve unless there was a man in the house. I believe that if you were around for me, I would have turned out a little better.
>
> What kind of problems did you have that kept you away for so long. Three out of 13 years is all the time I remember us being together. I missed out of all the things that other kids did with their fathers.

Do you think this inmate would have responded to the refuge and security of a home with boundaries? From talking with him and listening to his sense of loss, the answer is *yes!*

Setting boundaries will give your children a sense of esteem:

- belonging—security and identity; the knowledge that there is a place where they are loved and are supported for who they are
- worth—affirmation as a person of value; cherished and respected as an important family member
- competence—a sense of achievement; affirmed as an able person

Give the gift of protection by setting boundaries.

HOME: A PLACE WHERE YOU'RE SAFE, A PLACE OF REFUGE.

THINK IT THROUGH

1. Which of your parents' rules for you can you remember vividly?

2. What rule or guideline taught you the most when you were young?

3. What kind of discipline did your parents use most often with you?

4. When did you get together regularly as a family when you were young?

5. What disciplinary methods do you find to be most effective?

6. At what time each day is your family together?

7. When would be a good time to schedule a Family Council?

8. What would you like to cover at your next Family Council meeting?

   Check out these related Bible passages:
   Deuteronomy 4:9-10; 1 Samuel 3:11-13; Proverbs 3:11-12; 13:24; 22:6; Ephesians 6:4; Hebrews 12:5-11.

CHAPTER 3

Model Values

WITH eyes full of wonder, the little boy watches Daddy intently, his eyes fixed on each razor stroke that breaks a path through the heavy, white foam. Then as his father holds the razor under the hot-water faucet, he sees the used lather and cut whiskers swirl around the sink and swoosh down the drain. Afterward he feels Daddy's cheeks. Almost like magic the whiskers have disappeared. The boy also wants to shave . . . to be just like his father.

In another home, the scene is repeated with a mother and daughter. Carefully observing each stroke of the hairbrush, the child knows that someday she will fix her hair and dress just like Mommy.

Whether they like it or not, and whether they try to or not, parents exert a tremendous influence on their children. Subconsciously, kids copy Mom and Dad: their mannerisms, speech patterns, habits, and values. If you want evidence, think back to your grade school, junior high, and senior high years when your parents would scold you or discipline you and use such well-worn phrases as: "When I was your age . . . ," "After all I've done for you . . . ," and "I'll give you something to cry about!" Remember? You swore that you would never say such things; instead, you would be a kind, gentle, and patient parent. Yet, just the other day during a verbal sparring match with a child, one of those phrases tumbled out of your mouth. And you thought, *Where did that come from? I don't believe it—I've become my father!*

The most critical area of parental influence on children is *values*. Recently there has been much debate about "traditional values" and "family values." But what are values and why are they so important?

What Values Are

Simply defined, the word *value* means "having worth or importance." Although often used as an adjective (as in "a valuable possession") or as a verb (as in "I value my freedom"), the word *value* has gained importance as a noun (as in "values are important"). Used this way, a value is something or someone that has worth to an individual. And to "devalue" something means to reduce its worth or importance.

Values are significant because they form the basis for how we act. Our values determine how we invest our time and money, where we focus our attention and energy, and how we treat people. Our values influence how we understand right and wrong.

God's Values

God's Word clearly spells out what we should value. Just look at the Ten Commandments: the first four focus on making God the number-one value or priority in our life by honoring him and worshiping him alone; the last six focus on how we relate to others, beginning with our mother and father and then moving out to other relationships (see Exodus 20:3-17). Jesus summarized and affirmed these priorities when he said: "'Love the Lord your God with all your heart, soul, and mind.' This is the first and greatest commandment. The second most important is similar: 'Love your neighbor as much as you love yourself'" (Matthew 22:37-39).

In reading Scripture, we discover other values: human life is valuable because God created human beings special and in his image (see Genesis 1:26-31); family is important as the basic building block of society—people are to care for family members (see Ephesians 6:1-4 and 1 Timothy 5:3-5). Other biblical values include loving God's people (the church), reaching out to the poor and needy, telling people about Christ, taking care of one's place of worship, and being a good citizen.

THE WORLD'S VALUES

Unfortunately, the values in our world are just the opposite because God is totally neglected and individual rights take the spotlight. The world's overriding value can be summarized by the statement "Look out for #1." In other words, it's everyone for himself! If you want to do something, do it. If you have an urge, follow it. If you have a need, fill it. Do what feels good! This philosophy, clothed in the guise of "freedom," leads to moral bankruptcy and the devaluation of human life.

Check out the news. Daily headlines scream of senseless violence and murder. A 14-year-old boy from Massachusetts killed a

Buying is more important than giving, having is more important than being part of. It often seems that the sterile ceremonies of consumerism are the most profound rituals Americans share as a people. These values questions—about how we've chosen to live our lives and how that's affected our children . . . have been quiet American obsessions for some time now, the source of a deep, vexing national anxiety.
Joe Klein[1]

friend with a baseball bat "just to see what it was like." Afterward he walked to another friend's house, got into a snowball fight, and then offered to show his buddy the body. A psychiatrist who testified at the trial said that the boy was not conventionally insane. "He just doesn't know internally right from wrong. He knows the theory, but he can't perform the action. He is morally handicapped."[2]

Shocking stories like this, of course, aren't normative for all American kids. But they do illustrate the challenges we face as parents. And they led the *Washington Post* to conclude:

> While the severity of actions ranges from simple cheating at school to pushing drugs to cold-blooded murder . . . the depth of the problem has reached a point where common decency can no longer be described as common. Somewhere, somehow . . . the traditional value system got disconnected for a disturbing number of America's next generation.[3]

Time magazine asserted: "Ethics, often dismissed as a prissy Sunday school word, is now at the center of a new national debate."[4] But there's no debate in Proverbs 10:9: "The man of integrity walks securely, but he who takes crooked paths will be found out" (NIV).

For parents, this crisis of values is not a marginal issue pursued by moralists and leftover Puritans. It is central to the health and success of our children. It is also central to the health and future of our families. The issue of *values* is not a distraction from our more real and pressing concerns, such as purchasing a new car, or working an extra job to get ahead or buy some of the things we want. This issue of teaching children right values is more real and more important and will have a long-lasting impact on our children and their children.

Dad, your attitude, beliefs, and actions are much more important than the type of house you live in, the kind of job you have, or the amount of money you make. Who and what you value are more real and have more impact than what you *say* you believe. And values that are not rooted in an absolute God are only as good as those who hold them. Without firm, biblical values, our children become confused and anxious over the array of alternatives. If everything is of equal worth, the process of growing up becomes extremely difficult.

TEACHING VALUES

We convey our values by how we live. A person's values can be determined by watching where he invests his time, money, energy, and interest. Do you value your new car? Sure. Someone can tell by watching the way you take care of it, making sure it is protected from the elements and daily wear and tear. Do you value that old lawn mower? Nah. That's obvious by the way it sits in the corner of the garage, infected with rust and covered with cobwebs.

> Values that are naturally lived by people we watch become more a part of our soul than those values we are specifically taught. And my parents consistently and unselfconsciously modeled that relationship is the center of life.
> *Lawrence J. Crabb, Jr.*[5]

Do you value televised football games and other sports? Regardless of your denials, if you spend every spare moment glued to the set, your time and attention testify otherwise.

Now let's move the discussion one step closer. How much do you value your job? Is your work more important than your marriage, children, or church? Most Christian men would respond, "Of course not!" But what does your life say? Do your actions belie your words?

VALUING THE PERSON

Let me tell you what I (Chuck) value. I'm a runner. Running has been part of my schedule for more than 25 years. Throughout those years, I've competed in many races, including a few marathons. To complete a 26.2-mile race requires three months of intense training. My usual running schedule, however, includes Mondays, Wednesdays, and Saturdays. Because good running shoes can make or break a runner, I take care of my shoes. I have a good pair and a rain pair. If you were to observe me over a few weeks, you would see, by how I spend my time and how I take care of those shoes, that I value running.

My sons know that I run for three reasons: first, for my health; second, for the release of stress, to work through problems, and to think through issues; third, to discipline myself—I run regularly, rain or shine, hot or cold, convenient or not. But the boys also know that regardless of how much running means to me, they mean so much more. As Craig and Brian were growing up, they knew that if they had a ball game or another school event, even though it would conflict with my running time, I would be at the event. My presence spoke louder than any of my good intentions ever would.

> What are the social consequences of a cultural ethos that refuses to celebrate, among its various and competing norms of masculinity, the ideal of the man who puts his family first? Surely this missing language—this cultural black hole where the ideals of husband and father ought to be—helps explain today's shocking rise of fatherlessness.
>
> **David Blankenhorn[6]**

I have been involved with each boy since first grade, so when Brian played football for Wheaton College (in the Chicago area), I didn't consider it an inconvenience to attend his games even though our home is in Minneapolis. I didn't realize how important my attendance was to Brian until I overheard him talking to a teammate after a game during his junior year. I had been out of the country and had arranged my return flight to include a five-hour layover in Chicago. After jamming my luggage into a locker, I took the CTA to a terminal and then transferred to a bus in order to get to the game. I didn't think it was a big deal, but I heard Brian relating every detail to his friend. I realized how much Brian valued my efforts and my presence. Making the extra effort to be at Brian's games demonstrated that I valued him a great deal.

Unfortunately there are many opposite examples. One girl wrote:

> I hadn't seen my mother since she left me when I was four. Well, I did see her for 10 minutes on the street when I was 14, but we didn't know what to say to each other.
>
> So much anger and bitterness had built up inside of me. Over the years, she would occasionally send letters to my brother, sister, and me. Mom made promise after promise. But that's all there was between us—unkept promises.
>
> In one letter, she promised to take me out to lunch. I was six at the time and hadn't seen her for almost two years. I was so excited when my sister read the letter to me. Every day after school I would wait by the window for Mom to drive around the corner. After several months of waiting, I figured out that Mom wasn't coming for lunch or dinner or ever.
>
> Courtney Baldwin[7]

Do you value your wife and your marriage? Do you value each child? How are those values reflected in the way you spend your time and where you focus your attention? Of course you probably will spend more time at work than in any other single activity. Most jobs require about 50 hours a week, and often you won't have much choice in how much time you spend at work. But think about when you do have the choice and the areas over which you do have control. You may have to give up a favorite pastime, hobby, or leisure activity to spend time at home. You may have to leave the extra work at the office to be able to focus on your family. You may have to arrange your schedule around your wife and kids.

Do you want your children to value respect for the opposite sex, love for one's spouse, and the inviolability of marriage? Let them see that modeled in your life. Do you want your children to feel important and to value their own children someday? Let them see that modeled in you. By the way, if you want to find out whether your oldest child *feels* valued, ask. Go ahead—risk it. Remember, what your children perceive is more real to them than the fact that you said it.

VALUING INTEGRITY

Most Americans would agree that the American way of life and liberty stands on a commitment to individual integrity—people working hard, earning their wages, being honest and fair in the marketplace, showing compassion to the needy, and being good neighbors and citizens. So the question arises: Are we passing on those virtues to our children?

Historian Russell Kirk states:

> What gives a man dignity, and what makes possible a democracy of elevation, and what makes any society tolerable, and what gives just leaders their right to office, and what keeps the modern world from being Brave New World, and what constitutes real success in any walk of life, is private moral worth.[8]

Our children's character gives strong indication of our future as a culture. But think about it—the reason our kids are confused about morality is because society has tried to eliminate right and wrong and the stabilizing belief in an absolute God. As we remove God and moral standards from society, we will witness ever-increasing moral pollution in our families, schools, and even churches. "We laugh at honor," said C. S. Lewis, "and are shocked to find traitors in our midst."[9]

The most effective way to teach our children integrity is to model it for them. Do you value integrity? How do your kids know? Hopefully they see it in the way you keep your word, obey the law, and are honest in your dealings with others.

An evangelist was the featured speaker for a series of evening meetings at a church a couple hundred miles from his home. One day the evangelist decided to take the bus to a shopping center on the other side of town. He boarded the bus, handed the driver a dollar, took his change, and headed for a seat near the back. As the man looked at his change, he noticed that he had been given 10 cents too much. He wondered what he should do. The bus was filling with passengers, so it would be awkward to make his way to the front. And the bus driver probably would have to fill out a

Even when families remain intact, moral instruction is not automatic. A public school survey in Maryland showed that parents spent an average of 15 minutes *a week* in "meaningful dialogue" with their children—children who are left to glean whatever values they can from peers and TV.

I recently saw an article about the day care on Capitol Hill. Because, among so many couples in Washington, both husband and wife work, they have set up their own day-care center. A child is brought in at 7:00 each morning—just after he wakes up—a parent will often pick him up after work at 8:00 P.M. or 9:00 P.M. each night, just after the child has gone to sleep. The center also provides day care for vacations and weekends, making it literally possible for a couple never to see their child awake.
U.S. Senator Dan Coats[10]

form or something. It seemed like a lot of trouble for 10 cents. But eventually his conscience won out, so he wove through the crowd back to the front of the bus and got the driver's attention at the next stop. "Excuse me, but you gave me 10 cents too much in change," he said, handing the driver the thin, silver coin.

"I know," said the driver. "You see, I've been coming to the meetings at the church where you are speaking. I heard what you said, but I wanted to see if you were real."

As the bus lurched forward and the evangelist steadied himself for the rest of the trip, he felt sick to his stomach as he thought of how he almost hadn't returned the money. One thought continued to churn through his mind: *I almost sold out Christ for a dime.*

Unfortunately, many Moms and Dads sell out every day by their example. Consider the lesson children learn about obeying the law as they watch their father adjust the radar detector so he can speed and not get caught. Think of the lesson they learn about telling the truth when they hear Mom make up an excuse to miss a church committee meeting. And what do they learn about honesty when Dad goes through the tollbooth without paying? Those may seem like small and almost insignificant actions, but they speak volumes and teach values.

While taking his freshman daughter to the dentist, a father accidentally drove off the road and hit a tree. He responded by

> Take a man's personal performance under stress. I have noted fathers who have an unyielding conviction about maintaining family devotions seven days per week, but who can dissolve in unrestrained anger because a neighbor's untreated dandelions blow seeds over the fence and onto the front lawn. What about the father who demands perfect attendance at Sunday school but loses all control of himself when someone cuts him off in a traffic flow? Which behavior pattern speaks louder? Which will be more remembered? Which is more liable to be copied?
> **Gordon MacDonald[11]**

saying, "That tree is a hazard to drivers and should not have been there." In effect the father was saying that it wasn't his fault that he had hit the tree. His daughter was very upset and had this to say about the incident: "If I lied like that, my dad would have had my head. He lectures me on integrity and honesty, but he won't admit he is wrong. I was there and saw it happen!"

Kids learn integrity at home, from watching Mom and Dad.

VALUING MORALITY

A few years ago, "Just Say No" slogans began to pop up on bumpers and bulletin boards. That was a national campaign to motivate students to reject drugs and drinking. Because it's tough to say no to moral temptations that come from peers, especially friends, the campaign wanted to empower kids to resist peer pressure—and it was packed with good intentions. The problem, however, is that everything—from television ads, soap operas, and sitcoms to popular songs and the foul-mouthed disc jockeys who play them—seems to scream, "Just say yes!"

Even more disturbing are parents who say one thing and then do the opposite. You can talk with them at neighborhood parties and see them at the school activities. With cigarettes and drinks in hand, they bemoan the antics of their trouble-some teens. And many are quick to tell an off-color story or flirt with their neighbor's wife or husband.

Our children watch us carefully and notice our actions and reactions. If you want your kids to have certain moral standards, live by those same standards yourself. This includes the TV programs you watch, the videos you rent, and the movies you see.

The topic of morality also spills over to how we treat others. As Christians, we profess to follow Christ, to embrace the Golden Rule (Matthew 7:12), and to love people (1 Corinthians 13). Consider the example you are setting in your relationships. If you want your children to respect others, you need to model respect. The same is true for consideration, service, and love.

If you say that you value morality, then live morally.

VALUING GOD

We've already seen that the most important and significant biblical value is to "love the Lord your God with all your heart, soul, and mind." Having God at the center of our life means praying to him, reading his Word, spending time with other believers, and sharing our faith with friends and neighbors.

The importance you place on spiritual issues as the servant-leader of your home will influence your children's view of God for a lifetime.

During the past few years, I (Dave) faced the death of both of my parents. Those were very difficult experiences for me, but they also provided opportunities for remembering and reflecting. I knew that Mom and Dad had Christ at the center of their lives because Christ was at the center of our home. We prayed as a family, went to church as a family, sang together at church functions as a family, and often had devotions as a family. My parents were committed to church—we went just about every time the doors were open. Mom and Dad served on boards and committees, supported missionaries, taught Sunday school and Daily Vacation Bible School, opened our home for church socials and visiting missionaries and speakers, sang in the choir, tithed regularly, and served as youth sponsors. They actively participated in Youth for Christ and in other Christian organizations in the community. It's no wonder that I share their commitment to the church—because I know it's biblical and right, but also because I saw it in their lives. My brother Paul remembered often seeing Mom on her knees, praying for us.

As spiritual head of the home, fathers should take the lead in spiritual matters (see Ephesians 5:21-33). In many homes, however, fathers have abdicated all responsibility for spiritual nurturing to mothers or youth workers. Being the spiritual leader means initiating times of family prayer and Bible reading, working hard at applying Scripture to life, praying consistently for the children, keeping the family's priorities straight, and insisting on going to worship services together as a family. How important are Sunday school, worship, and other church activities? If you find it easy to skip the services because you're tired or you want to watch the big game on TV, your kids will copy your example. Remember, too, that preparation for Sunday's worship should begin on Saturday night—don't expect to be awake and alert on Sunday if you've been up till midnight the night before. Some families insist that everyone (even teenagers) is home by nine on Saturday night so they can get ready for church.

> Even when you are not consciously trying to influence your children, you are still doing it. What you say is not nearly as effective as what your child learns by observing you. The best thing you can possibly do for your children is to be a godly example. Let them see Jesus in you and they will learn to love your Lord.
> *Clyde M. Narramore*[12]

If you say that you value God, then live like it.

Having read this far, you might feel overwhelmed with the list of changes you should make and the things you ought to do (and there are eight chapters to go). You may wonder if anyone could possibly keep up with all the "shoulds" and "oughts"—who has the time? But most of these changes involve attitude and focus; it's not an endless to-do list. That's the case with transferring values to our children. As you try to keep Christ at the center of your life, he will change your desires and then give you the power to live as he wants (see

Philippians 2:12-13). Undoubtedly changes will have to be made in your lifestyle—hard choices such as turning off the TV so you can talk with your daughter, giving up that tennis match so you can make your son's recital, or skipping the bowling league this year so you can teach Sunday school at church. But those choices won't seem as difficult when you consider the goal—building solid, biblical values in your children.

There is no better way to foster values in the family than for fathers to nurture their children. That must be our first goal. Dad, your family is more important than your job. You can be very successful at work and a failure at home. Tragically, if that happens, you will deprive your children of the resources they need for the rest of their lives. Our character is at issue, and our children's future is at stake.

HOME: A PLACE TO LEARN WHAT IS REALLY IMPORTANT IN LIFE.

THINK IT THROUGH

1. What values did you see modeled in your parents' lives?

2. What was the strongest value you learned by watching how your parents lived?

3. In what ways do God's values conflict with the values of the world?

4. What values would you like to pass on to your children?

5. How do your children know that you value them as individuals?

6. How do they know that you value integrity?

7. What moral standards do they see in your life?

8. What would your children answer if asked, "How important is God to your dad?"

9. What changes do you need to make in your lifestyle in order to model the right values?

Check out these related Bible passages:
Deuteronomy 6:4-9; 11:18-21; Psalm 112:1-2; Proverbs 10:9; Matthew 22:37-40; Mark 8:36-37; 1 Timothy 5:3-8.

CHAPTER 4

Be Available

WHEN you hear the names Denise, Vanessa, Theo, Rudy, Claire, and Cliff, what family is probably being described? That's right, the Huxtables—from the long-running TV series "The Cosby Show." This hit program reached an unprecedented level of popularity, not only because of the charm and comedy of Bill Cosby and the humorous situations depicted, but also because people liked the Huxtables. The family stood together, with the parents in control, and the children, though very normal, listened, learned, and matured. Most significant, however, was the availability of the father, Dr. Heathcliff Huxtable. Whether celebrating Theo's wrestling prowess, working with Rudy on an assignment for school, or confronting Vanessa about drinking at a party, Cliff was always there. Viewers loved seeing a father who could take the time to be a dad. To many, Cliff Huxtable epitomizes the ideal father: tough but tender, firm but flexible, loving, compassionate, fun, and *always available.*

Many men object to the father example presented in the

show because the demands and pressures of work pull them out of the house and away from the family. In their reality, Mom has to deal with most of the stresses and strains of growing up, since Dad is home only before and after work and on the weekends. But that line of reasoning can also be a cop-out for not spending time with the family. Children need time with their fathers. Dad, your time is a gift only you can give, and it's a gift that money can't buy.

QUALITY VS. QUANTITY

During the past decade, much has been said about "quality time." The point usually being made is that a parent's mere presence means very little; it's the *quality* of the time spent at home that counts. The caricature is of a father buried in a newspaper or glued to the game of the week on TV—he's home physically but not emotionally; he sits isolated, inaccessible to anyone, especially children. In contrast, quality time involves personal interaction, reading to small children, playing with kids, solving problems, and teaching.

Undoubtedly parents should spend quality time at home— simply being there is not enough. Robert works from his house about three days a week, so he could legitimately boast of spending twenty-four hours at home each of those days. But eight of the twenty-four are at night when the family's asleep, and nine or ten more hours are during the day when the kids are at school or in extracurricular activities. That leaves six potential hours for interpersonal interaction. But if Robert immerses himself in the newspaper during breakfast while everyone is hurrying out of the house, pops out of his office for dinner, and then plops in front of the television until bedtime, he will spend virtually no quality time with any member of his family during the entire day. The quantity at home will be high, but the quality with the children, nil.

Quality time is important and necessary. But a dangerous flaw lies hidden in this line of thinking. It gives the impression that quality time is possible *without* quantity time. Having heard all of the talk about quality time, a father might assume that he doesn't have to be home very much as long as he makes the most of the time that he's there. So countless numbers of fathers rationalize putting in extra hours at the office, on sales trips, at conventions, or on the golf course with the excuse that they will give the wife and kids undivided attention when they're home . . . or they'll make up for their absence during the fabulous vacation week . . . or they'll have a heart-to-heart talk with the teenager on Sunday afternoon after the football game. But it doesn't work that way.

> I have come to believe that most adolescent boys can't make use of professional counseling. What a boy can use, and all too often doesn't have, is the fellowship of men—at least one man who pays attention to him, who spends time with him, who admires him. A boy needs a man he can look up to. What he doesn't need is a shrink.
>
> *Christopher N. Bacorn*[1]

Dad, let's say you have a spare hour on Thursday evening that you've decided to spend having quality time with your sixth-grade son. You approach his room and knock on the door. There's no answer. So you knock louder—you know he's in there because you can hear movement. Still no response. Finally you open the door and burst into the room. There's the boy, lying on his unmade bed in a pile of tapes and teenage trash, listening to his Walkman with his eyes closed, strumming an imaginary guitar. Would that be the time for an in-depth discussion of preparing for adolescence? Obviously not. Quality time only happens when *both* parties are ready, not just one.

Quality time is virtually impossible without quantity time. Absent fathers who breeze in and out of their children's lives seldom get to share in moments of joy, to comfort in times of sorrow, to counsel in crises, or to take advantage of teachable moments. Quality time begins with quantity time—you don't have to be Cliff Huxtable, but you do have to be present.

BE THERE

Dad goes out of town all week, but he showers everyone with gifts upon his return. At birthdays and Christmastime, he buys extravagant presents to assuage his guilt. The gifts are fine, but all the gifts in the world won't be able to make up for an absent or uninvolved father. When it comes to lack of time spent with the kids, the numbers are numbing. Research reveals a high correlation between homes disrupted by a father's absence and just about every social problem.

> When you comin' home, Dad?" "I don't know when. But we'll have a good time then, son. You know we'll have a good time then."
>
> *Harry Chapin, Cat's in the Cradle*

Many of the studies analyzed families in which the father was totally absent; in other words, the home had been broken because of divorce, desertion, or death. According to research by Karl Zinsmeister of the American Enterprise Institute, more than 80 percent of the adolescents in psychiatric hospitals come from broken families. Approximately three out of four teenage suicides occur in homes where a father has been absent.[2]

For 30 years, a study by the University of California at Davis tracked every child born on the island of Kauai, Hawaii, in 1955. The study found that five out of six adults with criminal records in this group came from families where fathers had been absent. The same study found that teenagers who had serious delinquency records or emotional problems were far more likely to straighten out as adults if they had grown up in a two-parent family.

In addition, the ability to learn is critically impaired in boys who grow up without fathers. A study by the National Association of Elementary School Principals indicated that girls from intact low-income families performed better on cognitive tests than boys from broken high-income homes.[3]

Other studies show that children from fatherless households (regardless of their ethnicity) are more likely to live below the poverty line, drop out of high school, use drugs and alcohol, commit delinquent acts, and score lower on standardized tests.[4]

How much does a father's presence mean? Here's how one boy expressed his feelings:

> When my parents told my 15-year-old brother and I that they are getting a divorce it hurt. It hurt a lot cause of the 12 years I have been living, only 6 years have been with my whole family and that's when I was younger.
>
> My father means a lot to me. I love it when he takes me places like basketball and football games. And some of our vacations have been special to me too.
>
> I like it when he tells me stories about his past. He never knew who his real father was or his name. Although his stepfather has been a great father to him cause I can tell from a line he says a lot, 'I hope I'm as good a father as mine was for me.' And he has. Everybody in my family has had to put up a lot with all the things that have gone wrong, or not exactly in the best way they could have gone. Sometimes he just says good-bye and walks out, and it hurts a lot. Sometimes I want to just cry. I wish this never happened, but it did and I know my family will never be whole, but I will always love my father a lot.
>
> Mark, sixth grade

The fact is that in the United States only 39 percent of children born in 1988 will live with both parents until their 18th birthday. Don't fall on the negative side of that statistic—your kids need you.

Economic realities force many families to work very hard to make ends meet, and many employers exert great pressure for business trips and overtime. But despite the demands of a job, each father has a certain amount of discretionary time to spend as he sees fit. So ask yourself what you can and should do to spend those hours at home, with the family. You may have to cut back on the golf game or give it up entirely for a while; you may have to reduce your involvement in community or social activities; you may have to turn off the TV; you may even have to turn down a promotion that would increase pressure and time commitments along with the pay. Spending time at home with your children is that important.

BE THERE AT BEDTIME

One thing about this divorce is that when I go over to my friend's house to spend the night, their father usually comes in and talks to us and says, "good night," not "good-bye." When my father comes over to get something, and he is about to leave, he always comes over and kisses me on the cheek and then says "good-bye," and walks out. If he would just be there when I go to bed.

Meghanne, sixth grade

One of the most important times to be home is bedtime—you can review the events of the day and pray together with each child. Bedtime is one of the most unguarded times in the day for children. When a child is young, this time can be ideal for answering questions and for listening to new words learned and experiences of the day that, if not reviewed, will be lost in life's busyness.

My sons saved up questions for me (Chuck) for bedtime. I heard of humorous events and even times of pain that I would never have been aware of if I had not set time aside to be with them. Those moments seem so very short as I reflect on them now, but sometimes it was such an effort to get to their rooms. Often I thought that I had more important things to do—church meetings or work that couldn't wait till morning. But I couldn't have been doing anything more important than spending time with my children. It made a difference in their lives then, and it makes a difference in my life now.

When I started being there for their bedtimes, I would sit on the bed, listen carefully, hug and kiss them, and then tuck them in. As they got older, I would sit in a chair. When they were teenagers, I would sit on the floor or lean against the wall. The hug and kiss survived the years, but somewhere we lost the tucking in. Just the other night, my youngest son came in and lay down on top of the covers between my wife and me. Brian hasn't done that in a very long time. He began to recount many of the special times we spent together at bedtime. He said, "When you came to my room at bedtime, it

> There is a capacity which must be mastered in the classroom of the family. Call it the teachable moment. We rarely *create* them; rather we *sense* them. The intellect of a child has doors like the entryways of a building. A teachable moment happens when that door has, through some circumstance, been thrown open. Fathers learn that the signals of a teachable moment vary with each child. For some, the signal is seen in a wistful look on the face; for others, it begins with certain kinds of questions. Don't overlook the "captive-audience moments" at the table, in the car, and in the moments just before bedtime.
> *Gordon MacDonald*[5]

was very important to me because it made me feel like I could talk about anything and you really would listen."

Being with children at bedtime is a wonderful tradition they will look forward to each day and cherish. It's never too early to start, and the tradition can continue into the high school years. Children take great comfort in the regular routine of their fathers.

Chris Kidwell explains:

> I go to all four of my kids' rooms each night to talk and pray. We'll work through struggles in math, or problems with a friend, or maybe we'll just have fun. This routine takes me about an hour and a half each night. But I know how important it is, and I love it. Even my 15-year-old son will come into my bedroom and hug me good night. I hug my daughters as well. I believe that a girl who receives a healthy amount of affection from her father won't need the boy in the backseat of a car.

The morning also offers great opportunities to spend time with kids, especially when they're younger. Little children tend to be early risers, so you can help get them up and ready for the day (if you don't have to rush off to work).

Sometimes it was 7:00, but often the cry would come earlier, intruding into my (Dave's) last hour of sleep. "Daddy, come and wake me up!"

Usually it took only one call. But if I didn't respond, the message would be repeated, loud and clear: *"Daddy, come and wake me up!"*

I would walk across the hall to Dana's room, peek around the door, and see my three-year-old so proud in her grown-up bed, pretending to be asleep. Then I'd lightly kiss her "awake."

She'd flash open her bright eyes, wrap her little arms around my neck, and give me a big hug and kiss.

Sometimes I'd surprise Dana with tickling, and she'd tickle me back between giggles. Soon we'd be laughing and hugging and tickling.

Sometimes, I'd walk in the room and mumble just loud enough for Dana to hear and understand as she hid beneath the pink blanket: "Hmmm, I don't see Dana. She must already be up. I guess I'll just sit here on this lump in the bed. . . ." Then slowly I would lower my weight onto her legs. She'd squirm out of the way and I'd move, and soon her squirms and giggles would get both of us laughing. Then she'd give me that wonderful Dana-hug again. It would be a great morning!

We played that game, day after day, for two or three years. I never tired of it. Gail would tell me how disappointed Dana was when she'd call out and I couldn't come because I was out of town. That was a daily, special time we shared.

Now both of my daughters are teenagers, but we still try to get together in the morning, even as they rush off to school. And when I remember, I'll write notes of encouragement and slip them into my girls' lunch bags. Recently both Dana and Kara told me that they have saved most of those notes.

The beginning and ending of each day provide golden moments with children. Be there.

BE THERE WHEN THEY HURT

Hurts take many forms and always arrive uninvited and unexpected. Ted was cut from the sixth grade basketball team; Melinda's best friend called her a name and made fun of her on the playground at recess; Kris was so nervous for her solo in chorus that her voice cracked three times as she performed; little Stephanie has battled the flu for three days; Julio feels like an outsider at his new school; Jason is afraid of the bigger boys in the neighborhood; John is devastated after being dumped by his girlfriend.

What would happen if the truant fathers of America began spending time with their children? It wouldn't eliminate world hunger, but it might save some families from sinking below the poverty line. It wouldn't bring peace to the Middle East, but it just might keep a few kids from trying to find a sense of belonging with their local street-corner gang. It might not defuse the population bomb, but it just might prevent a few teenage pregnancies.

If these fathers were to spend more time with their children, it just might have an effect on the future of marriage and divorce. Not only do boys lack a sense of how a man should behave; many girls don't know either, having little exposure themselves to healthy male-female relationships. With their fathers around, many young women might come to expect more than the myth that a man's chief purpose on earth is to impregnate them and then disappear. If that would happen, the next generation of absentee fathers might never come to pass.

Christopher N. Bacorn[6]

When children hurt, they need someone to hold them, to listen, to offer encouragement, and to give help. Being available when children hurt means more than physical presence; it means being open, sensitive, encouraging, and helpful. Unfortunately, there are many examples of the opposite reaction from fathers:

- "Don't bother me now. Can't you see I'm busy?"
- "Now what are you crying about?"
- "It's no big deal—you'll get over it!"
- "If you had listened to me, you wouldn't have this problem."

Jesus used the example of good fathers to explain the love of the heavenly Father for his children: "Which of you, if his son asks for bread, will give him a stone? Or if he asks for a fish, will give him a snake? If you, then, though you are evil, know how to give good gifts to your children, how much more will your Father in heaven give good gifts to those who ask him!" (Matthew

7:9-11, NIV). Good fathers give good gifts. We may find it difficult to identify with stones and snakes, but we give similar "gifts" when we are insensitive to our children's feelings.

When your child is hurting, drop what you're doing and *listen* to his story and his pain, *empathize* with his struggle and fears, *hug* and *encourage* him, *remind* him of your love and support, *offer counsel* and advice. Don't belittle, condescend, repeat clichés, or say, "I told you so."

Let your children know that even if you're not with them physically, you wish you could be there and are with them emotionally. On business trips, call home every night and, after talking with your wife, speak with each child individually. Ask about the child's day and listen for hints of hurts.

Explain to your children that they can even call you at work if they have a problem or a concern. Tell them that, if possible, you will interrupt what you are doing to talk with them.

Be there when your children hurt. They need you.

BE THERE WHEN THEY FALL DOWN

Jeremy comes running into the house with his hand on his bleeding knee, tiny tears streaming down his little face. He has fallen on the sidewalk and skinned his knee. He wants to be comforted, to be held. Suddenly Jeremy's knee feels much better when Mommy kisses it to make it well.

Physical nosedives are not our kids' only falls. As much as we would wish otherwise, like their parents, children are not perfect, so their lives will be filled with mistakes, setbacks, failures, and sins. And when they fall, they need us to pick them up, give them a hug, dust them off, and set them gently on the right path.

In chapter 2 we discussed the importance of setting boundaries—rules, regulations, and guidelines. These boundaries help to provide a sense of security in children and to develop self-discipline. But setting the boundaries is only half of the process—the boundaries must be enforced. In other words, our children need to be told when they're off course, out-of-bounds. When they slip or stray, they need to be firmly yet gently corrected. But we can't help them if we're not there.

Many dads have trouble with this aspect of fathering. Some cop out and leave the nurturing and the discipline to Mom. Others blow up at the slightest infraction, taking the act of disobedience or the youthful mistake as a terrible personal insult. But think about it—do you really love your kids? Of course you do. Is there anything they could do that would cause you to stop loving them? Of course not. So the real issue is knowing how to react when our sons or daughters fail, defy our authority, or run into trouble.

We can't cover every topic in great detail in this book, so we won't give detailed instructions on how to react in every family emergency. The main point, however, is that fathers need to be there for their kids, especially when they fall. Perhaps the greatest service you can render during times of personal crisis is loving acceptance. At times a hug is all it takes to reassure your son or daughter of your love. You approve of the person even if you object to his or her behavior.

Shelley broke the CD player by using it after she had been told not to; James was threatened with suspension by the principal for fighting on the playground; Deron received an *F* for math this quarter; Alicia got caught shoplifting makeup at the drug store; Mom found a stack of *Playboys* under Mike's bed; Bob crashed the station wagon; Susan is pregnant. I'm sure you can imagine other "falls." You may not be able to be there in person, every time, for every fall, but you *can* be there emotionally—dropping everything, when necessary, to come home.

Your children need you, so be there when they fall.

Love is spelled T-I-M-E. The father's presence makes a difference. Here's a word of caution: if you decide to begin spending time with your kids, they might not want to right away because they're not used to it. But don't give up—they'll soon warm up to having you around.

Dad, you have to be home, for quality and quantity time, at bedtime, when your children hurt, and when they fall.

HOME: A PLACE WHERE DAD CAN BE FOUND. A HOUSE HAS AN ADDRESS; A HOME SHOULD HAVE A DAD.

THINK IT THROUGH

1. What does this statement mean: "You can't have quality time without quantity time"?

2. What do you remember about bedtime when you were young?

3. What occasion do you remember where your father was there for you when you hurt?

4. In what ways were your parents there for you when you experienced failure?

5. How can you rearrange your schedule in order to spend more time at home?

6. What bedtime ritual can you begin with each child?

7. What recent hurts or failures have your children experienced where you could offer support, comfort, and encouragement?

Check out these related Bible passages:
Deuteronomy 6:4-9; Psalm 103:13; Proverbs 3:21-24;
Matthew 7:9-11; 1 Corinthians 13:4-6; Hebrews 13:5.

CHAPTER 5

Listen with Understanding

WHEN my (Dave's) daughter Kara became a teenager, an amazing transformation occurred. Kara began talking incessantly on the phone and stopped talking to me . . . or so it seemed. One incident in ninth grade stands out in my memory as typical of our "conversations." While driving her home from school, I decided to converse.

Question: "How was school today?"

Answer: "Fine."

Question: "How did volleyball practice go?"

Answer: "Good."

Question: "Do you have much homework?"

Answer: "No."

Obviously the discussion had stalled on one-word answers. But then I thought, *Wait a minute! I write discussion questions for a living. I know I can do better than that!* So mentally I constructed a great question, one that I was sure could not be answered with a simple yes or no or with a short retort. I can't remember the question, but you can be sure it was a good one, asking for an explanation and delving into feelings.

Still she answered with one word. I gave up, and we drove home in silence.

A few days later, I served as designated chauffeur for Kara and her friends, driving them to and from a school event. As I drove from house to house, the noise level in the car increased with each new passenger. They talked about everything—school, boys, friends, "stupid" teachers, "Beverly Hills 90210," who was going out with whom, homecoming, makeup, and other teenage concerns. All the girls, including Kara, spoke freely—as though I were invisible! I listened quietly . . . and learned about their lives.

There is a time for listening.

Learning to listen to children is one of the most important skills any parent can learn. But it's tough for adults to listen carefully to children—we'd rather talk, give advice, pontificate, make a speech, state our opinions. When we listen, however, we demonstrate acceptance and concern for the child, we give permission to the individual to contribute to our knowledge and understanding, and we learn. And, by the way, our kids know when we listen, and they appreciate it.

One father told about a lengthy discussion he had with his son about their relationship. When the boy explained that Dad did not always treat him fairly, Dad asked him to write out what he thought were the most important attributes of a good father. To the father's surprise, his son was gone less than 10 minutes, returning with a long list. Guess what topped the list:

> Listen to both sides of an argument, and respect the opinions of the other person.

The father explained: "Over the past four years, I have looked at the list several times and felt that for a lad in the tenth grade, he showed a great deal of insight. I now realize that learning to listen was the turning point in our relationship."

Many children really believe that their fathers will not or cannot listen with understanding. (This is especially true after seventh grade.) But listening *with understanding* can make a great difference in a relationship, and it's a gift we can give that money can't buy.

LISTEN TO WHAT THEY SAY

Effective listening begins with giving our children a hearing. Remember, God gave you one mouth and two ears: perhaps that means you should listen twice as much as you speak. Obviously we communicate with our mouths; but the communication process must also involve our ears, to receive messages.

Remember when someone asked you a question but then had his or her attention diverted as you were giving your answer? The person's excuse, "Sorry, I wasn't listening," didn't make you feel any better, did it? Or how do you like it when someone interrupts you by saying, "Excuse me, you were saying . . . ?" Or how do you feel when the person you're talking to is constantly looking around?

That should give you a glimpse of how children often feel. We can be so busy or preoccupied that we don't *hear* them.

Listening seems so simple, but actually it is complex and challenging. If you think it's easy, try holding a conversation with someone in a room with the TV on. Place yourself so that the other person can see the TV but you can't. It'll drive you crazy because the person's attention will be diverted constantly by what is happening on the screen. Now think of what competes with your children for your attention: pressures at the office, bills, deadlines, phone calls, home repairs, special events, sports, the newspaper. . . . How do you think they feel?

One large obstacle to effective listening is a lack of willing-ness to sacrifice time. My (Chuck's) oldest son was five years old when I made an agreement with my wife that I would not participate in a sport that my children could not be involved in. So my golf game suffered because I didn't play for about 10 years. Was it worth it? Here's what my son wrote at age 23:

> Thanks for taking time out for me when I was little, for being at my Pee Wee and Little League games, good weather and bad. Our once a month get-out-of-school lunches were great. Your volunteering to work at school events made me feel important. It meant you really cared. It was super then, but even more important to me today because I am beginning to understand what it meant to you to commit time out of your schedule for my needs. Thanks for being there for ME.

Being a good listener begins by examining your priorities. What is most important to you as a father? Is work more important than your relationship with your son or daughter? This means listening when it is not convenient to you or your schedule. It means putting down the newspaper for 90 seconds to give time to your questioning four-year-old who wants a little of your time before he's off to the next interest in his life. With small children, get down on their level to look in their eyes, or bring them up on your lap. Those "sacrifices" seem awfully small when compared with what your time means to your kids.

Make listening an integral part of your routine. Carve out a time to be alone with each child on a regular basis. Try to sit down with your nine-year-old after school and hear about all that has gone on during her day. Sometimes it will seem as though she won't ever quit talking; on other days she won't have much to say. Take your son to the store, even when it's easier to let someone else take him. You will learn much about what he is thinking by listening to him while you're there. Here's another suggestion: take your teenager out to dinner—that will be a special event for both of you. Dinnertime can also be a great opportunity for conversation. Think through possible topics that would interest your children, and invite them to offer input.

Take every opportunity to listen to your children as individuals . . . to what they have to say. Listen with your mouth shut and your mind open.

LISTEN TO WHAT THEY MEAN

Taking time to hear what children say—their words—is the first step. But effective listening goes deeper. We also must listen to what they mean.

I (Chuck) remember an incident that taught me that listening is more than just hearing. Have you ever brought work home from the office that distracted you from truly listening to your children? That happened to me once when Brian was in junior high. While working on a project, I muttered a response to something he was asking me about. I didn't give much thought to it until I overheard Brian tell his mother that I had agreed to buy him a new pair of $40 Guess jeans. When it comes to money issues, I normally am aware of what I am agreeing to buy. But not that time. I had heard Brian ask the question, but I hadn't listened very carefully. I had heard him speak the words, but I hadn't caught the meaning. It took me a long time to live that one down.

> It is impossible to overemphasize the immense need humans have to be really listened to, to be taken seriously, to be understood.
> *Paul Tournier*[1]

Listening means getting the mind involved. Unfortunately, however, much of our listening is passive: we hear words and sounds, but we don't absorb them. If you don't think this applies to you, ask your wife what you are like at the dinner table after a hard day at work. You may be there physically, but are you there mentally and emotionally?

Vicki Grossman, a family therapist in Bothell, Washington, and cofounder of the Youth Suicide Prevention Center, says that her most important piece of advice to parents is to "listen actively." She lists five guidelines for active listening (this is her list with our explanations).

1. *Hear your child out.* Don't rehearse in your mind how you will answer your child. Instead, listen carefully to what is being said and evaluate the child's requests when he or she is through talking. It takes self-control and humility to avoid making judgments, especially when your child's views contradict your own. But hear the child out and then give your honest appraisal. Proverbs 18:13 says it well: "He who answers before listening—that is his folly and his shame" (NIV).

2. *Keep your eyes on your child.* Have you had a conversation with someone who rarely looked you in the eye? You probably felt as though the person wasn't really interested in what you had to say. If that person was your boss or supervisor, you may have felt belittled or insignificant. Think of how your kids feel. Remember, they see you as a very important person in their lives; you can make them feel good or rejected.

Building self-worth in your children begins by letting them know that you see them as individuals of value. This means giving them your undivided attention when you are talking to them or listening to them. Look at your child when he or she is talking to you. Gazing around the room, at the TV, or out the window is distracting and implies that you are not listening. Even if circumstances are such that you can't maintain eye contact, let the child know that he or she still has your attention.

3. *Create an atmosphere of acceptance.* When children don't feel threatened, they are more likely to share their anxieties as well as their fun experiences.

When I (Chuck) was working with inner-city teenagers in Detroit, I had many opportunities to see how teens will open up when they don't feel threatened. Rodney was a 14-year-old kid who didn't trust anyone. Busted by the police three times, he had been in and out of group homes since he was 11. I met Rodney at our summer camp. At the camp dinner table, Rodney wouldn't even pass the milk because he thought he wouldn't get a second glass if he didn't hang on to the carton. It took from Saturday, when he arrived, till Wednesday for him to feel safe enough to begin to tell me about his home life and when he first got into trouble at school. I had to establish a climate that showed I really cared about him, so I didn't laugh or put him down for his past.

What made the biggest impression on Rodney? The fact that I looked at him every time I talked with him. At first he would only glance at me once in a while. Then, as he felt less threatened, he would look me in the eye. As I got to know Rodney, I could see fear in his eyes—he searched my eyes to see if I would betray him like so many others had in the past. As the week went on, he shared more and more of himself. Several years later, he told me that the week at

Last winter my dad and I drove my sister out to college, and on the two-day drive back we just talked. About everything. He is the best listener and he never talks down to me, like some adults do. I talked about school, my goals and friends, the latest boy I was interested in, and my feelings about life, religion, and our family. Not once did he tell me my thoughts were wrong. He just listened and expressed his point of view.

Twelfth-grade student

camp was the beginning for building his self-worth. The key to Rodney was showing that I cared. I communicated this by looking at him even when he wouldn't look at me.

Creating an atmosphere of acceptance also means not interrupting or contradicting your child when he or she is speaking to you. Make your child feel comfortable by giving all the affirmation you can. Positive gestures like smiling and nodding often will prompt children to keep speaking. And don't make fun of your child, even if he or she is very young. You may be tempted to mock a preschooler for his or her dramatic or pitiful appeals, but don't do it. Children are people. Creating an atmosphere of acceptance means taking them seriously.

The place is also important. Your son may feel more at ease talking about school issues while shooting hoops. Your daughter may be able to share her dating concerns while the two of you are biking.

4. *Force yourself to be interested.* Parents often tune out their children because it seems too tiresome to listen to all the details of their activities or because children don't know how to express themselves well. When she was quite young, my (Dave's) daughter Dana loved to tell Gail and me about a show she had seen on TV or something that had happened during the day. But inevitably she would get so caught up in the details that soon we'd be lost. It was very tempting to interrupt Dana or to cut off her spiel—it took great patience to hear her out.

I (Chuck) remember being home one evening with my youngest son, Brian, when he was three. My wife was out for the evening. I was reading a book that really had my attention when I realized that for some time Brian had been calling from his bedroom, telling me that he was feeling sick. He had become more specific and told me that he was going to throw up. Still absorbed in my book, I mumbled something to the effect that he was OK and not to think about it and he would be all right. If I had just forced myself to listen to what he had been saying earlier, I would have heard the growing intensity in his voice—but I didn't. Believe me, I wish I had listened earlier as he threw up all over the floor while standing on his bed.

When you force yourself to listen, you may be surprised at all the delightful and not so delightful things you can learn. You may also perceive emotional, social, and spiritual needs that you may not have discovered if you hadn't listened.

LISTEN TO WHAT THEY FEEL

This is Ms. Grossman's fifth point: *Listen to feelings.* To listen with understanding to our children, we must listen to what they say and we must listen to what they mean; but we must also listen to what they feel.

In addition to the words used, feelings may be shown through body language and tone of voice. A shrug of the shoulders can communicate more than a hundred words. A sigh does not always mean disagreement; it can be an unenthusiastic yes to your request. The way your children sit or stand speaks volumes about their attitude. If you don't hear their feelings, you will miss where they are, what they are going through, and what they really mean by their words. A child walking home from school, slowly, with his head down, shuffling along, may be daydreaming and simply taking his time. But it also may be that he is upset over something that happened in class or on the playground.

Notice the tone of your child's voice. Is she angry or upset? Is she hesitant and afraid? What's going on beneath the words, on the inside? The way the words are spoken can provide clues. And if your son or daughter stops talking altogether, he or she may be going through tough times or a serious struggle.

Work at becoming a student of your child and his or her style. Then you will be able to spot his or her needs and struggles. Remember that each child is different, and each will express his or her emotions in a unique way.

> I don't know what it is to have a father. I see people that have one, and I wish I had mine. I've always wanted to feel the love of a father. Sometimes my days are bad and I cry because I need someone there to talk to, to share my troubles, my fears, and most of all my dreams. I've been through a lot of bad moments and if he would of been there, none of this would have happened because he could have been there to protect me. I feel empty inside.
>
> **Twelfth-grade student**

Of course, after you have listened carefully and have determined your child's feelings, the next step is to respond. Be careful here, especially if your son or daughter is upset. A brief word of encouragement accompanied by a touch on the shoulder will communicate your care and concern and may open the floodgates of tears or anger. Sometimes, silence is the best response, especially when it is clear that your child doesn't want to talk right at that moment. Beware of giving a speech or of insinuating "I told you so." That may make you feel better, but usually it won't help the child or the situation.

> The 14-year-old daughter walks through the door.
> "How was school today?" asks Mom cheerfully.
> "Great . . . just great," she replies tersely as she drops her books on the kitchen floor and slumps into a chair.

As an objective witness to that scene, what feelings do you hear in the daughter's response? Consider the way she spat out her words, what she did with her books, and her body language. Obviously something's not right. What do you think the mother should do next? What would you do or say?

Now think of your own son or daughter. Can you read his

or her emotions? What would you say to a son after a heartbreaking loss on the basketball court? How would you respond when your daughter seems hesitant about accepting a friend's invitation to a party? What would you do after your child stomps upstairs and slams the door to his or her room? Learn to listen to the emotions; then you will have a better idea of how to react.

A RETURN ON THE INVESTMENT

If you take time to be with your children, learn with them, and listen to them, you will receive a large dividend on your wise investment in their lives.

First, you will relate to their real needs and help them where they need help. You will give them a gift that they will appreciate. They will love you for it.

Second, you will become closer to them. They will see that you care and that you really understand what they're going through. When you listen to your children, you pay them a great compliment. You contribute to their feelings of well-being and self-respect.

Third, your children will learn how to listen by watching *you* listen. And if they copy your example, they will learn to hear you out. Can you believe it? Having won the right to be heard, you would have the opportunity to share from your wealth of knowledge and experiences.

Your investment in your children

Dear Dad,

. . . Even though you don't wear a suit and tie to work like Tommy's dad, I wouldn't trade you for anything. Tommy's dad brings work home from his office every night and even on weekends. They never go to the zoo or play ball in the park or go fishing off the pier.

I like the way you talk to me when I am down. You always make me see that things aren't so bad and that they will get better, which they always do.

. . . I like the way you tell me the truth about everything. When I grow up and have kids, I want to be just like you.

From a letter to Ann Landers[2]

will be a gift that will last them a lifetime—a memory of a father who listened.

HOME: A Place Where You Can Be Heard.

THINK IT THROUGH

1. When you were growing up, who listened to you with intensity?

2. Why is listening difficult to do?

3. Why is listening important?

4. What makes a good listener?

5. Recently, when have you listened intently to what one of your children was trying to tell you?

6. Which of these phrases best describe how your children perceive your listening skills?
   • "Dad hears what I say."
   • "Dad knows what I mean."
   • "Dad understands what I feel."
   Explain your answer.

7. In what ways do you need to improve your listening skills?

8. What can you do to become a better listener?

Check out these related Bible passages:
Proverbs 13:1; 15:1; 17:27-28; 18:13; Ecclesiastes 3:7; Colossians 3:21; James 1:19.

PART TWO

THE *gift* OF IDENTITY

Who are you? No, really—without using your name, how would you describe yourself?

Your answer might include your employment—a job title or line of work. Or you might respond by referring to your physical attributes. Or you could explain your various talents and abilities. Or you might discuss your family and friends.

That's your identity—how you see yourself—the personal qualities that you deem important and that give you a sense of worth. One man might answer: "I'm a sales rep. I'm 6′3″ and can play a pretty good game of basketball. I'm a Christian and very active in the church, where I sing bass in the choir. I'm also a father, husband, and son."

Someone else might respond: "I'm Irish through and through. I'm the father of two boys and one girl. I work at the Ford plant, where I'm a line supervisor. I enjoy softball and fishing in the summer and skiing in the winter. I'm 42 years old, six feet tall, and weigh two hundred pounds."

Those facts are important to us—they help define who we are.

But what if I asked you how you *feel* about yourself? Your answer to that question is critical and also ties in to your identity or self-concept.

How we see ourselves and feel about ourselves is important, affecting how we act, what we achieve, and how we relate. A man who hates himself feels worthless and may take out his anger and frustration on others. But where do those feelings come from? Where do they start? Where do we begin to form our identity anyway?

At home.

A child's first understanding of who he or she is comes from Mom and Dad. Sadly, the message that many kids hear at home is that they are worthless . . . and useless . . . and in the way. Instead, they should be learning that they are special, loved by God and family, invaluable, beautiful, precious, and talented. Those first messages, communicated verbally and nonverbally, mold delicate egos and propel them into the future. Parents exert a powerful influence here.

A good, healthy, and positive identity is a gift that you can give, and it's a gift that money can't buy: From Dad, with love.

CHAPTER 6

Accept Unconditionally

D ESCRIBING his relationship with a high school daughter, one father wrote:

> Jenni and I have had our struggles. Some of it is probably because we are so much alike. We're both strong-willed (that's spelled S-T-U-B-B-O-R-N). A few weeks ago, Jenni and I were finally uncomfortable enough that we were forced to talk it out. A lot of things we had not addressed over her 17 years, so we had many issues to discuss. I didn't realize that I had blown so many things for so many years. (Of course most of them were insignificant, and I have explanations for the rest . . . NOT!)
>
> The truth is that she never felt total acceptance from me. I can hardly believe it, her own father. I know how I feel about her, how proud I am and that stuff. Why doesn't she know it? It's mostly a matter of not saying it in her love language—with actions that really communicate my love and acceptance to her. We got a

lot of things cleared up during those two difficult days, and our relationship has never been better. We have a new appreciation for each other and a love that feels a lot more like love instead of the "I know I love you, but I'm not sure I like you" feeling.—Frank

The gift of identity begins with accepting children unconditionally. In other words, we need to love them without reservation, not because of their looks, intellectual capability, physical ability, gender, or performance.

AS GOD CREATED THEM

Remember when your child was about to be born? You probably were asked quite often, "Well, what do you want . . . a boy or a girl?" If you answered like most, you said: "We don't care if the baby is a boy or a girl, as long as he or she is healthy." That's a good response, but is it true? Some men long for a son and find it difficult to accept a daughter. Often they will let Mom rear her or turn her into a tomboy.

And do you remember sitting late at night, rocking your precious newborn to sleep, and imagining what he or she would become? Your dreams may have included physical characteristics ("Surely she will be beautiful—probably homecoming queen"), athletic accomplishments ("He's got the body of a linebacker— all-state for sure, maybe the pros"), artistic endeavors ("Listen to that voice—she's going to be a soprano like her mother"), academic achievements ("A gifted child"), or career advancements ("He'll take over the company"; "Millionaire"; "President of the United States"). Dreaming about the baby's future can be exciting—children hold so much promise and potential. But those dreams can turn into nightmares for the child when Mom or Dad pushes him or her to perform or pressures conformity to a preset life pattern or career path.

Comparisons with siblings exacerbate the problem. Imagine a family with two boys: the older one is shy, intellectual, and musically inclined, and the younger is extroverted and athletic. Which boy would tend to be favored by the father, a former three-sport man in high school and an All-American college athlete? Unless that mom and dad work hard at accepting and affirming their oldest son, he will feel invisible and worthless simply because he has different interests, capabilities, and motivations—not worse or less important, just different.

Accepting children unconditionally means accepting them as God has created them with no strings attached. This, of course, does not mean that parents should not discipline children, encourage them to develop certain skills, or challenge them to move out of their comfort zones. To let kids simply wander through life in any direction they choose at any moment would be irresponsible. Parents need to help children discover and develop their talents, abilities, and gifts. But that's much different from molding children into our image; in effect, attaching conditions to our love.

Accepting children unconditionally means being able to live with the fact that our sons and daughters aren't perfect and aren't the best at everything they do. Some children spend their entire lives trying to prove their worth because they never felt that they earned their fathers' respect, approval, and admiration. How do you react to your child's *B*-minus on the report card? If he has done his best, accept the fact that he may not be a straight-*A* student. How do you react to your child getting cut from the seventh grade volleyball team? If she really wants to play and you see potential in her, help her work on her skills and encourage her to be ready for the tryout in eighth grade. But be ready to accept the fact that she might not earn that volleyball scholarship to college in a few years, and help her channel her energies into a different area.

It hurts to watch our dreams crumble, but our acceptance of our children can help them mold their own dreams.

For children to know that we accept them for who they are and not for something they are not or someone we want them to be, they need to know our hearts. And we, as fathers, need to allow God to "turn the hearts of the fathers to their children, and the hearts of the children to their fathers" (Malachi 4:6, NIV).

IN LANGUAGE THEY UNDERSTAND

Ask yourself this question when communicating with your children: "Are they hearing what my heart is saying?" Unfortunately, the heart isn't always what they hear. Consider the situation described at the beginning of this chapter. Over those years, Frank certainly loved and wanted the best for Jenni, but he had missed her attempts to explain that she didn't feel accepted by him. His statement says it all: "I know how I feel about her, how proud I am and that stuff. Why doesn't she know it? It's mostly a matter of not saying it in her love language—with actions that really communicate my love and acceptance to her."

We may think that we have been quite clear in communicating that we accept our children, but a child may not receive that message. In fact, he or she may hear something quite different.

For example, a child may assume that you don't mean *him* when you express your love to the *whole family*. So this communication must happen individually. It's not enough to tell the family or the kids in general that you love and accept them. Talk to each child personally, in private, one-on-one, from your heart. No matter how often we express our love for *all* the children, a child may think, *everyone except me*. Unconditional acceptance is an individual matter.

Or consider the fact that our children hear us talk continually about how busy we are and that life doesn't allow us to do what we really want to do. Normally we don't mean that we don't have time for our kids, but often that is what they hear us saying.

Of course, sometimes we communicate mixed messages because our actions belie our words. That is, we may say that we accept and love a child and then act the opposite—we vote with our feet. As explained in chapter 4, love is spelled T-I-M-E. You may say, "I'm very proud of you, Susie. You look beautiful in your ballet outfit. And you are such a good dancer." But if Dad can't find time to go to the ballet recital, Susie probably will not believe his words.

This has been a tough lesson for me (Dave) to learn. I see myself as an athlete, having played football and basketball in high school and football in college. For several years after college, I played basketball just about every weekend in the winter for several years. About ten years ago, I became a runner (I've finished five marathons). I love sports—participating, coaching, observing, cheering. Yet God has blessed me with two daughters. Yes, they are athletic, but they'll never catch a touchdown pass or make a bone-jarring tackle in football. Over the years I've attended countless gymnastics, dance, piano, and voice programs and recitals, and I've cheered at volleyball games, swim meets, and soccer games. Even though my interests had been in other sports, my higher priority was to make sure my daughters felt loved through my attention to their activities.

D**arryl Savage has his priorities straight. He's making a career change because the exciting life of a TV reporter was taking too great a toll on family life. "This job has been so hard on my family, my baby, a 9-month-old baby. I'd be working late and get home just in time to see him fall into deep sleep. And I just thought, 'You know, this is not what life is about.' . . . Five years from now when he comes home with a big grin on his face and says, 'Dad, will you come to my kindergarten play tomorrow?' I couldn't live with myself if I had to say no."**
Minneapolis Star Tribune[1]

For our children, the perception that they are loved is much more important than our words or other "evidence." Although you provide a home, food, clothes, spending money, and a yearly vacation, that won't cut it with your kids if they don't *feel* loved. On the other hand, children who do feel loved have a much better chance of succeeding in life than those who don't. According to John A. Wood of the Southern Baptist Convention's Christian Life Commission,

> The single most influential factor of adolescent behavior
> is the young person's perception of being loved.
> Research reveals that those youth who see their parents
> as loving and providing freedom within guidelines
> are not prone to severe problems.

The question is this: If our children need to perceive that they are loved, how do we give them that perception? How do we speak in language that they understand? We climb the steps.

STEPS TO ACCEPTANCE

To help visualize the process of expressing unconditional acceptance to your children, think of a set of stairs. We need to start at the bottom and climb one step at a time.

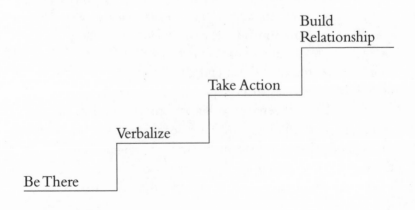

Be There

By now you surely have heard the message that your presence is requested and strongly urged at home. You won't communicate to your children that they are important to you if you are absent. They will feel that if they're not important enough to bring you home, they're not important at all.

That's the first step. The gift of your presence means more than any expensive toy or creature comfort. Listen to this story of three teenage girls who didn't outlive their parents' absence.

> The six high school students often partied at Katherine Macaulay's gated home overlooking a golf course in an exclusive neighborhood of Pasadena, California.
>
> This party began as many others apparently had, with a case of beer, a bottle of whiskey, and perhaps some drugs. But by the end of the evening, three teens had been shot to death at point-blank range with a 12-gauge pump shotgun, and two boys had fled to Oregon in a Mercedes-Benz. A third boy stayed behind, promising to cover for them.
>
> A week after the slayings of Katherine Macaulay and Heather Goodwin, both 18, and Danae Palermo, 17, friends and neighbors described them as ordinary teenage girls who liked to listen to heavy metal music, who were not interested in school, and whose plans barely reached beyond the upcoming prom. One neighbor described Katherine as a friendly girl with plenty of spending money who had simply fallen in with the wrong crowd.
>
> "Why a girl that comes from a professional family like this, why she should get involved with some of the weeds of humanity, I just don't understand it," said Mark Russek, a retired neighbor. "She was in bad

company for the moment, which she may have gotten past, but this tragedy just struck before she outlived it."[2]

As you read reports such as this one, don't you wonder where the parents were? Where was the father when Katherine got "involved with some of the weeds of humanity"? Of course, not every teenage daughter who doesn't have her father around when she needs him will end up murdered. And not every girl from a wealthy home who has been given money and things by her parents instead of a relationship will turn to a wrong boyfriend for her self-worth. But it happens.

Children need their fathers to be actively involved in their lives. When Dad's not home, a child will go to great lengths, and sometimes extremes, to have his or her love-hunger met, even through counterfeit love. Contrary to what their neighbor believed, Katherine had been in bad company for a great deal longer than a few hours. And it was just a matter of time until things fell apart. Some kids don't outlive bad fathers!

> A father's lack of connectedness to his children also opens the door for a child to experiment with numbing agents such as drugs or alcohol. To bridge that gap, fathers have to learn to recognize and express their feelings.
>
> *Margo Maine*[3]

Acceptance begins with your presence. Let your kids know that they hold a higher priority in your life than the activities jamming your schedule.

Verbalize

Let's assume that you love your children and that you spend time at home with them. The next step is to tell them—to verbalize your feelings.

The lament is repeated again and again by grown men: "Dad never told me he loved me." Age has little to do with the need to be loved.

Some fathers deny that they need to say "I love you." But children have a strong need to hear it continually. Can you identify with these comments?

> He never told me he loved me. I just knew he did, but I needed him to tell me just once. He kept his love bottled up inside and said he couldn't say it. It felt like my father wanted me to earn his love. I'm 52 years of age. I asked my father to tell me he loved me. His answer was, "I can't."

After I (Chuck) had finished conducting a seminar one January in Grand Island, Nebraska, Mark, a 27-year-old father of two, told me about his experience with his father. He explained that the previous fall, for the very first time in his life, his father had shaken his hand and had told him that he liked him. It was such an emotional experience for Mark that he was unable to work for two days. One reason it was so traumatic was that Mark could not remember his father ever touching him before that day.

At another seminar, a mother shared her concern for her three sons. Early in the discussion, it was very evident that her boys had little or no relationship with their father. One son had dealt with the problem better than his two brothers. The oldest boy had the most difficulty with his distant and absent father. As a junior in high school, this young man was the last child to be with his father as he lay dying of cancer. The son's only request to his father was, "Tell me you love me!" His father refused. The son has not recovered from that rejection. Some of the negative characteristics that he so despised in his father are appearing in his own lifestyle, and he has begun to abuse alcohol and drugs.

Your words of acceptance and love can have tremendous power in your children's lives. Speak them.

Take Action

Actions affirm acceptance.

Four-and-a-half-year-old Mikie's dad had promised to play catch with him and to teach him how to catch a ball. But for two weeks, Dad had put off fulfilling this promise. Again Mikie asked his father when they would be playing catch as he had promised. His father replied as he had the week before, "Son, we will do it tomorrow." In exasperation, Mikie blurted out, "Daddy, you really don't want to teach me to play ball. You just think you do!"

Dad's actions spoke volumes to Mikie about the relative importance of playing catch with him. If this pattern of rejection continues, what kind of relationship do you think Mikie and his dad will have when Mikie is 10? This father's actions will push Mikie away, convincing him that he is not important to his father.

Spending time with children should begin when they are born. Apply the sports cliché "No pain, no gain." Most fathers find it difficult to alter their busy schedules and leave important responsibilities to meet a young son or daughter's needs. They'd rather let Mom handle it. Some men don't enjoy taking care of an infant—changing diapers, feeding, pushing a stroller, playing games. It takes a decision and commitment to do that messy and time-consuming work. Taking time away from other activities may be "painful," but the gain in the bonding with that child will be worth it. In fact, a dad can learn to enjoy his baby if he holds him or her at least five times a day.

Child development experts stress that a child's personality is mostly formed by age five or six. Unfortunately, some fathers don't start trying to connect until their children start school or are old enough to play games—usually soccer, catch, basketball, baseball, and so forth. Although it's never too late to get involved, fathers should begin to develop meaningful relationships with their children at the earliest ages.

In addition to spending time with them, "taking action" means taking the initiative in determining our children's interests and abilities. Through an elementary school teacher, one father learned that his son was becoming quite proficient on the computer. So he allowed his son to use the computer in his office at home, and he took the boy to a computer store to pick out some software. Another father encouraged his daughter to try out for a solo in the school talent show; then he spent time working with her on what she would sing for the tryout and helped her rehearse for the show. In both cases the dads were accepting their children for who they were—finding their strengths and building on them. We will discuss this further in chapter 8.

Back up your words with positive actions. Taking the initiative to determine your children's strengths and to spend time with them will help demonstrate that you accept them unconditionally.

Build Relationship

The final step is building a growing relationship with each child. Become friends.

Think of your closest friends over the years. What cemented the friendships? An important factor for most solid friendships is a spoken or unspoken promise to each other—a commitment that the person will be there for you no matter what you say or do. That's unconditional acceptance.

In reality, it's also the foundation of our friendship with God. Think about it. God accepts us unconditionally; we don't have to dress up for him or become something we're not. Of course, there is a difference between acceptance and approval. God doesn't approve of everything we do; in fact, he *hates* our sin. But God loves us. We know that God accepts us unconditionally because he is present (see Psalm 139:1-18; Romans 8:38-39), because he tells us (see John 14:1-4; 1 John 3:1; 4:7-8), because he acted and continues to act on our behalf (see John 3:16; 1 John 4:9-12), and because he sticks with us (see Deuteronomy 4:31; Hebrews 13:5).

Building a relationship with a child, therefore, is the ultimate step in the process of accepting him or her unconditionally. You spend time with the child; you express your love for him or her; you demonstrate your acceptance and love by your actions; and you stay close in every circumstance.

Do your kids know they are accepted by you even when they do the dumbest thing in the world, like drop a light bulb or spill a glass of water (and they are teenagers)? It's when your children do the little things right or wrong that you can let them know you accept them. When your kids make mistakes, you need to confess that you, too, have done stupid things. If you don't talk about your own struggles, they will have no way of knowing that you have feelings and hurts just like they do.

How do you respond when your kids really blow it—when they fail in a big way, let you down, disappoint you, or hurt you deeply? Do you still love them? Of course you do. But do you accept them and work to put the pieces back together? That's the kind of commitment it takes to build a relationship.

Suggestions for Dad:
- Spend time with your daughter. If Dad takes time out of his schedule, that gives the message that she is a worthwhile person.
- Starting at an early age, let your daughter spend time with you while you are doing "masculine" things. Let her help out.
- Take her to your workplace.
- Watch television with your daughter and point out the way programs and commercials stereotype women.
- Encourage her nontraditional as well as traditional interests. If she wants to get involved in sports, go to her games.
- Tell her she is beautiful, or she looks nice.
- Don't criticize her weight or appearance.
- Continue to expect good grades.
- The bottom line is, whatever you would do for your son you should do for your daughter.
  Patty Carney-Bradley[4]

Building a relationship also means allowing our children to accept us. When I (Chuck) have really blown it with my sons, I tell them I'm wrong and ask for forgiveness. Most of the time, they accept me. But even if they don't, I know that my Father in heaven will accept me regardless, even with my failures and my inability to meet the needs of my kids. Then, as God accepts me unconditionally, I can pass on his grace to my children.

Strong relationships also feature a healthy give-and-take—communication and leadership don't always go in one direction. Applying this principle to the relationship between a father and a child means that, as the child grows and matures, the father and child become more like peers, on the same level. As babies and toddlers, children have no choice but to take direction from above.

As children get older, however, they should be moving toward maturity and independence from Mom and Dad. Finally, as late teens they should own their behavior and take full responsibility for their actions. Where do your kids stand on the growing-toward-maturity continuum? Can you accept the fact that they are growing up? That's part of unconditional acceptance.

KEEP CLIMBING

Accepting children unconditionally is a continual process—we climb the steps every day. Children are constantly growing and changing. What seems to work one week with one child may fail miserably the next week. If you have more than one child, you may become very confused when you find that what worked with the first child leads to disaster with the second. In addition, what works with a quiet, compliant child seldom works with an outgoing, assertive, strong-willed child.

Regardless of the differences among children or their stage of development, we must keep climbing with each of them—

spending time, telling of our love, acting in love, and allowing the relationship to grow.

Climbing the steps seems to be exhausting. Is it really worth the effort? You bet it is! Accept your children unconditionally. Give them the basis for holding their head high, confidently stating their existence. That's a gift that only you can give, Dad, and it's a gift that money can't buy.

"I AM."

THINK IT THROUGH

1. With which of your parents did you get along best? Why?

2. When you were growing up, how did you know that your parents loved you?

3. Why is it important to accept children as they are?

4. What makes it difficult for you to accept your children's feelings?

5. What can you do to show each of your children that you love them unconditionally?

6. List three ways that you can show love to your children through how you spend your time.

Check out these related Bible passages:
Psalm 139:1-18; Malachi 4:6; Mark 9:36-37;
Romans 8:38-39; Hebrews 13:5; 1 John 4:7-12.

CHAPTER 7

Affirm Worth

I (DAVE) was 18 and about to embark on a new stage of life—college. Mom and Dad had driven me to the campus and had helped me get settled in the dorm. The next day I would leave for football camp. The time had come for them to leave . . . for me to be on my own. We didn't voice all of our feelings, but we knew that things would never be the same. Mom gave me her usual warm hug, kiss, and assurance of her love before she got in the station wagon. I walked back around the car and, for an awkward moment, stood alone in the street with Dad—father and son, man to man. Then he spoke words that I will always remember: "Thanks for being a good son and for being such a good example for your brothers and sister." His eyes filled with tears; he shook my hand; he got behind the wheel; and he drove away.

That experience is forever etched in my memory because of the powerful words of affirmation and the emotion with which they were spoken. Dad carefully guarded his feelings— seldom had I seen him cry. And yet he told me, with tears, that

I was good. Of course there had been many affirming words along the way—about sports, music, even grades—but those meant the most.

When we affirm our children, we assure them that they are all right, and we help build their self-esteem. Affirmation goes one step beyond acceptance; it says, "You're good!"

Unfortunately, contemporary society is replete with examples of neglect and abuse. Pick up today's paper—you'll find a story or two. More and more children are growing up in homes where the only contact with their parents is negative. Typical communication includes phrases such as: "You _____ kid—can't you do anything right?" and "You idiot!" Through the string of expletives, the message is heard loud and clear: "You are no good—worthless!"

Children have become expendable, marriages are not for life (only till things get tough), and being married isn't fun. Parents abuse children because they themselves were hurt and abused. They arrived on the parental scene with no good techniques or models, unsure how to pass on values to children when they had not been valued.

> I am the father of a son. I want to teach my son how to be a good person. But while that is necessary, it is not sufficient. I also want to teach my son how to be a good man and how to be a good father. But when I look around me for help and reinforcement in that crucial task, I see a culture that, at its best, communicates confusion, fear, and anxiety on the entire subject of what it means for a boy to become a man. At its worst, I see our culture as actively hostile to this entire enterprise.
>
> **David Blankenhorn**[1]

In sharp contrast stands Jesus. Remember? He called the children to him and said, "Let the little children come to me, and do not hinder them, for the kingdom of God belongs to such as these. I tell you the truth, anyone who will not receive the kingdom of God like a little child will never enter it" (Luke 18:16-17, NIV).

Jesus made children feel welcome, and he validated their simple faith in him as Savior. Then he presented them as examples of the only way to receive the kingdom of God.

EXPECTATIONS OF CHILDREN

Many fathers consider themselves far beyond the tragic stories of abuse reported in the news. They would never harm or neglect their children. But through their absence and other subtle actions, they communicate a similar message. It doesn't take violent outbursts to tell someone that he or she is worthless. We can do it through silence and by withholding compliments and praise.

Often the problem stems from our expectations.

Russell Lund amassed a family fortune through his dealings in oil, gas, and real estate. He made his family name renowned throughout Minneapolis and St. Paul through a chain of upscale grocery stores.

With all of the affluence and success, however, Lund's only child, Russell Jr., floundered in life. Friends said that he was intimidated by his father's shadow and could never measure up to his father's expectations. As a young man, Russell Jr. took no interest in the family business. Instead, he concentrated on his hobbies—aviation and amateur radio—two areas where he found acceptance and worth.

Although we might have expected him to act differently with his own children, Russell continued the pattern set by his father. He was described by those who knew him as an often distant and unemotional husband and father. His passions in life kept him away from his children and home, physically and mentally. Russell Jr.'s life ended tragically—he took his own life in a hospital room after having been accused of murdering his estranged wife of 24 years and her boyfriend.

Don't you wonder how approachable Russell Lund, Sr. was

to his son growing up? Could Russell Jr. talk to his dad? Could he explain to his father how he felt about life? Did they spend much time together?

Evidently, Russell Jr. felt as though he never could please his dad. He always fell short of his father's expectations.

What do you expect of your children? Are your expectations realistic? Remember, there's a difference between encouraging them to do their best and holding standards that are impossible to achieve.

> Children need parents. They need to be loved. They need to be needed. They want to know that we care enough about them to give them some of that most precious commodity—time. We all must examine our schedules and see just how much of our undivided attention is dedicated to our children. There are times when we should let nothing else, mentally or physically, come between us and our child. It is only by spending time with our children that we really get to know them.
>
> *William Swindell*[2]

The highest prize in professional football is the NFL championship—winning the Super Bowl. For most owners, coaches, players, and fans, anything less is failure. So every year, only those associated with *one* football team, the champions, feel satisfied. The rest are losers. That's ridiculous, of course, but it's typical for Americans in many arenas. We want to be number one, and anything less is unacceptable. So we have pageants, bowls, cups, Emmys, Grammys, Oscars, Neilson, Arbitron, top 40, all-American, all-state, all-conference, honor rolls, Pulitzers, and on and on.

Parents sometimes project these cultural expectations on their kids—if they're not "number one," they're failures.

Instead, we should let our children know that second, third, fourth, honorable mention, and even "participant" are good too, as long as they've worked hard and done their best. And even when they haven't worked hard and they have done far less than they should have, we should affirm them as valuable persons. Their value is not based on their performance.

In the last chapter we discussed unconditional acceptance. This is where affirmation begins. Our children must know and feel that we love them just the way they are; that is, they don't have to change or perform to earn our love. Then, secure in their relationship with Mom and Dad, they can build their identity.

FEELING WANTED

One important part of acceptance is the feeling of being wanted. Not only does Dad accept his son for who he is, but Dad really wants to spend time with his boy. It's great knowing that someone wants to be with you and will even seek you out. And it hurts to see someone avoid you or simply tolerate you.

I (Dave) spend a lot of time with junior-high young people, at church and at the local middle school through Campus Life/JV. Often, early adolescents seem to be invisible in church. High schoolers often have a full-time youth minister to tend to their needs, and everyone likes working with the little kids. But junior highers fall in the middle—they're at the awkward age where they are growing and changing rapidly. They're just not cute anymore. I find that they really respond to an adult who welcomes them, who wants to spend time with them. They feel good, all right, OK, affirmed.

It takes work to make sure your children have access to you and your heart. Sometimes we seem too busy; sometimes we're not in the mood; at other times, the kids are a pain and we'd rather shut them out. Welcoming our children doesn't just happen. It takes resolve and work to move beyond good intentions. Does your son feel like an interruption? Or does he know that you really want to be with him? Does your daughter feel like an intruder? Or does she see you changing your schedule to spend time with her?

Over the years, I (Chuck) have tried several methods for staying approachable to my sons. Some worked and some didn't. One of the more effective ideas helped build their sense of worth and cost me only a quarter. When each boy turned 12, my wife and I marked it as a special event in their lives. One part of this rite of passage was to give the boy a quarter and a personal pledge. As I handed him the quarter, I said, "This quarter will get you to me anytime, anywhere. My secretary has been instructed to put you through to me whenever you call. Regardless of the meeting I'm involved in, you can have my attention. And I'll accept your collect call, regardless of where I am at the time."

I tried to choose a memorable setting for the quarter ceremony. For my oldest son, I chose a beach along Lake Michigan, one of his favorite places. Over the years each son took advantage of my offer and called about five or six times. They accepted the trust that I gave them and used it.

A larger benefit that I didn't see at the time was the gift of value and worth they received by my being accessible to them individually at their times of need. They felt wanted. Recently my youngest son told me how much that gift had meant to him. He mentioned that he had told several of his classmates at the time about the quarter his dad had just given him. But he also said that just one week ago, he had shared the story with a friend. Needless to say, his words brought a lump to my throat and tears to my eyes. I didn't have the privilege of that kind of affirmation when I was his age, and I'm grateful he has this heritage.

A child feels rejected by an absent or an emotionally inaccessible father. This inevitably breeds resentment and hostility. Several studies point to the same conclusions: absent fathers contribute to their child's low motivation for achievement, inability to defer immediate gratification for later rewards, low self-esteem, and susceptibility to group influence and juvenile delinquency.

In 1981, Armand N. Nicholi of the Harvard Medical School and Massachusetts General Hospital predicted that if the absent-father trend continued, the quality of family life would continue to deteriorate, producing a society with a higher incidence of mental illness than ever before. This illness would be characterized primarily by lack of self-control. Second, crimes of violence would increase, including violence within the family. The suicide rate would continue to rise, and we would continue to witness changes in the expression of sexual impulses.

> My dad "God blesses" us before we leave for school. Mom says he watches us walk to the school out the window until he can't see us anymore. She says he gets tears in his eyes almost every time.
>
> *Third-grade student*

Unfortunately, Dr. Nicholi's predictions were very accurate. In every category, the results have been even worse than expected. The future looks even more troubled if we can't reach dads with a positive model for fathering.

As we discussed in chapter 4, be available to your kids. And whether you're home or away, be approachable. Let your children feel wanted.

FEELING APPRECIATED

Many churches use "Affirmation Cards." Placed in the pew racks or on a table in the foyer, these cards encourage affirmation. Someone could write a thank-you note to the soloist for her special number. Another person might express gratitude to a Sunday school teacher for his faithful service. Someone else might say how much he appreciated an individual for her bright smile and positive attitude. If you've ever received a card like that, you know how good it feels. You feel noticed, complimented, appreciated, affirmed.

We're not suggesting that you send your kids cards all the time, although at times that would be a good idea. The point is simply that we should look for those ways; that is, we should try to catch our kids doing things right and then tell them so! "Thanks for setting the table. It looks great!" "I really appreciate the way you do your chores around the house without being told." "You have a great sense of humor!" "You really feel strongly about things that some people don't even think about. That's a gift." "You're special!"

We can communicate our appreciation in many ways.

Expressing appreciation also includes how we show our affection. Probably your kids know that you love them, especially if you've told them. But do they think you *like* them? There's a difference. Love sort of comes with the territory. Kids think, "Of course you love me. You're my dad—that's your job."

We've stressed many times already that an effective way to communicate love and "like" is by spending time with our kids. But another powerful way to show affection is through touch. According to medical studies, people who are touched frequently tend to have fewer illnesses, recover from sickness faster, and live longer. Babies who are given a lot of physical affection tend to show more rapid intellectual development than those who have been deprived.

"Skin hunger," the lack of physical contact, has a number of unhealthy results. Think back to the Romanian orphans shown on TV when the Communist government in Romania was overthrown. Their tiny bodies were ravaged by poor physical care and hunger, but emotionally they were also malnourished because they hadn't been touched or held.

Children need to be touched. In fact, some who lack physical affection will misbehave just so they'll be touched through spanking. This lesson was forcefully brought home to me (Chuck) when Brian was eight years old. It was one of those situations in which all the discipline tools in the kit had been used and the only one left was spanking. One of Brian's friends had come to the house and was waiting for him outside. After the spanking and our time of talking through the incident, Brian went out to his friend. Several days later, Brian told me that the subject of spanking had come up with that friend. Jeff had said, "I wish my dad would spank me." Brian had been surprised; he didn't know there were any kids who never got spanked when they needed it. So he had asked Jeff why he would say that. Jeff had answered: "Your dad loves you. My dad doesn't spank me even when I do something really bad. I don't think my dad loves me very much."

> Your message really hit home and as I was driving to my house afterwards, I began to cry and realize how much I had longed to be affirmed by my father. My father came from a broken home and as I was growing up he was never intimate or emotional with me. . . . Your seminar helped me realize how important this affirming and touching is to the development of my children.
>
> *A Kansas father*

Other research indicates that a father's active affection toward his children is the most important factor in shaping their sexual identity—for both boys and girls. The affectionate father is most likely to foster normal, heterosexual development in his sons. The lack of appropriate and affectionate touch during youth often leads to sexual promiscuity in adulthood. Girls with affectionate fathers are much less likely to become boy crazy in order to satisfy their need to be touched.

Guidelines for Touching

1. *Affection should begin with your wife.* Your children will benefit from seeing you kissing, hugging, holding hands, and touching Mom. And incidentally, mothers who give the most affection to their children tend to be those who receive lots of it from their husbands.

2. *Touching is critical for infants.* It's easiest at this stage to find ways to touch: holding, rocking, playing, bathing, and diaper changing are just a few. Be a participant, not a spectator. Dads who refuse to change diapers miss golden opportunities to bond with their children. Child rearing should be a team effort by Mom and Dad from start to finish.

3. *School-age kids enjoy physical play.* Get down on the floor and wrestle with them, or engage in a tickling spree. You could snuggle up together to read, brush hair, give back rubs, etc. Also, ritual affections, such as bedtime kisses and good-bye hugs, give a sense of security to a child.

These suggestions may seem elementary, but many dads have no idea of what they can and should do. A TV special sponsored by the National Center for Fathering featured a short segment in which a father was wrestling on the floor with three of his children. After seeing this, a man called to say that he had never seen a father wrestle with his kids. Then he asked if that was acceptable behavior for today's father. The answer is yes!

4. *Boys need affection too.* Adolescents, especially boys, may be reluctant to show or receive physical affection from Mom and Dad, but they still need it. Usually you can be creative or work out a compromise. For example, you might say, "I need a hug from you." Or you might agree just to touch him on the shoulder or shake hands when in public. It is very unfortunate that, in our culture, men are trained not to express their feelings or to touch their children. Yet in the world of sports we can give "high fives," arms around the

neck, and hugs. Watch the celebration after a hockey or soccer goal!

Hugging and displaying any affection was not part of my (Chuck's) heritage. My home broke apart through a bitter divorce when I was a sophomore in high school. My father abandoned us, ending what little involvement he had had in my life. Thus my childhood did nothing positive to prepare me for fathering. Through God's grace, a surrogate father came into my life when I was 14, and I was able to catch a glimpse of how a father should act toward his children. Until then I hadn't even known that fathers gave anything to their kids—I can't remember my dad giving me anything. I started to earn my own money in sixth grade, and I bought my first car in ninth grade (in those days, in Kansas, you could get a driver's license at 14).

Understanding my background, can you picture my re-action when my strong-willed, 16-year-old son drove me to the airport and then kissed and hugged me good-bye in front of everyone? I cried—and that was something else I didn't think I was allowed to do! This is a reward for the gifts you give that money can't buy—an indescribable, priceless gift from your child.

When Brian was a senior in college, Myrllis and I at-tended his last home football game. During half-time he was to receive his all-American football award. When his mother and I walked onto the field, Brian hugged and kissed his mother. Then he turned and did the same to me. I was blown away! I wept then, and I weep now as I write these words. It is only by God's grace that my son would give such a gift to his father. God intervened in my life with a substitute father, and my terrific wife taught me how to nurture our children. If I can learn to be affectionate with my sons, you can learn to be affectionate with yours.

You may avoid touching your daughters for fear that it might be improper. Sexual abuse is a reality, but most men know the difference between a fatherly touch or embrace and a sensual one. A daughter needs to be held, consoled, and touched by her loving father. If you avoid touching your daughter after her twelfth or thirteenth birthday, she might satisfy her need for touch by being touched inappropriately in the backseat of a car.

Kathy is 16 and struggling with what type of boys she thinks she wants to date. But an even bigger question for her is: "Why did my dad stop treating me like he did before I turned 13? It's like he's rejecting me because I'm growing up or something. He even stopped hugging and kissing me good night. I feel like I did something wrong. Maybe he doesn't like me anymore."

We can affirm our children's worth by helping them feel appreciated.

FEELING SIGNIFICANT

Children love to know that they have something to offer. When we take them seriously, we show that we think they are valuable.

A number of years ago, a fellow Youth for Christ staff member taught me (Dave) a lesson. Steve had graduated from seminary and was leaving to take a position with a church. At his going-away party he slipped me a note that read: "I will learn from you if I think you can learn from me." In a gentle way, Steve was confronting me with my arrogance. In our relationship and relative positions on staff, I wanted to teach him and give him advice. Yet I was closed to his suggestions. The teaching only went one way. The result was a lopsided relationship in which I was not allowing Steve to feel significant.

Parents love to give speeches, pouring forth profound

advice by the mouthful. And we get upset if our children fail to listen with rapt attention and follow through down to the smallest detail. Perhaps our children would be more open to learning from us if we were open to learning from them.

When we think of arguments, we often think of adolescents. They are moving toward independence, trying out adult roles, and throwing their weight around. And as they discover their minds and learn how to think, they want to challenge Mom and Dad intellectually, arguing about everything from studies to politics. It takes patience to listen quietly to teenagers' interesting opinions. The temptation is to argue and refute them at every point. But don't shut teens out with your eloquence or impatience. Be open. Take them seriously. Who knows, you may even learn something!

Even small children appreciate being taken seriously. Whatever you do, don't make fun of their attempts to offer advice or a possible solution to a problem. When I (Dave) was four years old, I awoke my father, who was napping on the couch. At first he was angry—until he saw the flames coming from the stove. Not all of your children's interruptions will be that dramatic or helpful, but listen to what they are saying. Children want to know that they have value, that they have something to contribute.

Help your kids feel significant.

> My dad was very busy when I was a child, but I could always manage to get his attention. I can still see him sitting at his desk during my preschool years. He was in the final year of his doctoral studies at the University of Southern California, and the pressures were intense. Nevertheless, my brother and I took priority. I would climb on the chair behind him and spend an hour or two on his lap or even on his shoulders. He never seemed to mind. Every now and then he would stop to toss me in the air or play a game. These moments, even more than gifts and surprises, were the way he expressed genuine love to this wide-eyed child.
>
> *Danae Dobson*[3]

FROM DAD WITH LOVE

A nurturing father reaches out—is proactive in offering affirmation or comfort. He takes the initiative in giving gifts that last. Accepting children unconditionally lets them know that you know they exist: "I am." Affirming their worth by helping them feel wanted, appreciated, and significant lets children know that you know they have value.

"I AM SOMEBODY."

THINK IT THROUGH

1. When you were very young, what caused you to feel insignificant and worthless?

2. What caused you to feel important and valuable?

3. What did your parents do to affirm you as a worthwhile person?

4. In what ways do our parents' expectations for us affect how we feel about ourselves?

5. How do your children know that they are wanted?

6. What can you do to show your children that you appreciate them?

7. What can you do with or for each child in the next week to affirm their significance?

Check out these related Bible passages:
Genesis 1:26-28; Psalm 139:13-18; John 14:1-4;
Romans 12:9-10; 1 Thessalonians 2:11-12; James 3:7-12.

CHAPTER 8

Acknowledge Uniqueness

THE most spectacular development in American business in the 1970s was the explosion of franchising, especially in the fast-food market. It began with McDonald's in the late sixties, but soon Kentucky Fried Chicken, Wendy's, Burger King, Pizza Hut, Hardee's, Taco Bell, Popeye's, Subway, and others appeared on every big corner. Today we have franchises for a dazzling array of consumer products and services. And they're successful: the failure rate for franchises is less than 10 percent, compared to independent businesses, where about 75 percent fail within the first two years.[1]

Perhaps the biggest reason for the success of franchises is consistency—customers know what to expect in the store. For example, with only a few variations, every Wendy's is the same: menu, prices, service, layout, decor, etc. And that could be said for the rest. When someone walks into McDonald's to order a Big Mac, he expects the sandwich to be exactly like the one he ate yesterday on the other side of town and the one he had two weeks ago on the other side of the world.

Sameness and consistency feel comfortable, and living seems easier when we know what to expect. It's also much quicker. If we shopped for all our groceries the way we choose produce, we'd be in the store all day. Instead, we look for certain brands and packages, and we drop them in the cart, trusting the truth of the packaging. We know this box of Wheaties will contain the same amount and same kind of crunchy flakes the last box had.

> I love him because he takes time to play catch with me. . . . I wish he could be home more. He works a lot.
>
> *Eric, second grade*

But people aren't franchises or products, neatly packaged with reassuring and predictable sameness. Each person is unique, "fearfully and wonderfully made" (Psalm 139:14, NIV). And that's certainly true of children. Much as we would like to be able to predict our kids' behavior, discipline them, guide them into the future, and so forth, they are different. Understanding, acknowledging, and appreciating the uniqueness of each child will help us be better parents and give our children the gift of identity—a gift that money can't buy.

FOCUS ON CHILDREN INDIVIDUALLY

Regardless of how many children you have eventually, the oldest one is an only child for a while, receiving attention, praise, and adoration. First-time parents awake suddenly with every nighttime whimper and rush to the doctor with each little cough, runny nose, or fever. With subsequent children, however, they tend to be much more relaxed and let nature run its course. Parents (and grandparents) also tend to lavish attention on the "baby" of the family, spoiling him or her with presents. So kids in the middle can feel ignored or forgotten. Regardless of where a child fits in the birth order, however, he or she needs personal attention from Mom and Dad. They need to know they are "that special."

When my boys were quite young, I (Chuck) made a commitment to meet with them once a week (four times a month). These get-togethers or "appointments" would last 45 minutes to an hour, depending on what we were doing that week. I attempted to spend two appointments a month on their life notebooks (explained in detail below). For one appointment, I would pick them up from school and take them to a fast-food restaurant of their choosing. The other appointment would be to do something fun with Dad—*alone*.

I remember picking up Brian to take him to lunch. I pulled up to the school playground, and before I could get out of the car, my excited third grader opened the car door and got in. I remarked, "Boy that was fast." And he answered, "Yeah, I know. I wanted the kids to see who I was going to lunch with." Then he rolled down the window and yelled good-bye to his friends.

> My dad plays with me and Melissa. My daddy loves me. He plays with me. I love my daddy. He takes me to the park. He takes me for ice cream. He takes me swimming. Dad always takes me on a date. He loves my mommy. My daddy means a lot to me. He takes me to Colorado by ourselves. Daddy helps me with my homework. He takes me to Florida. He likes to listen to me read my reading books. He plays baseball with me. He takes me on walks with my dog. He tickles me a lot. I love my dad because he is a Christian father.
>
> *Lauren, kindergarten*

We can't overemphasize the importance of "just you and me" occasions with each child, even though these times might be inconvenient. When a child knows that Dad loves him or her specifically, every day can become an adventure.

Spending time with each child communicates that he or she is an important individual, not just one of the kids.

TREAT EACH CHILD AS IMPORTANT

Even an only child needs to sense that he or she is important to Mom and Dad and to God. When Jesus was baptized by John, his Father said, "You are my Son, whom I love; with you I am well pleased" (Mark 1:11, NIV).

This process begins by teaching children to respect life. God created the human race, every person—each one is a unique creation of a loving God. Genesis 2 tells of God's special creation of Adam and Eve, the first human beings. Unlike the plants, animals, and all else that God had made, Adam and Eve were created in God's image and were given responsibility in the world. So human life—all human life—is valuable because of God. We also read in the Bible that God does not discriminate against people on the basis of race, nationality, or sex (Acts 10:34-35; Romans 10:12; 15:7; Galatians 3:28). We can model this value by accepting others and showing kindness to everyone—even those who cut us off in traffic!

In addition to the biblical value of respecting life, we should emphasize other teachings of God's Word that enhance our children's self-esteem. For example, Psalm 139 highlights the involvement of God in our lives even before birth. Romans 8:33-39 says that God is for us and that we can never be lost to his love. And, of course, the often quoted and memorized John 3:16 proclaims God's amazing love for us. God loved us so much that he sent Jesus, his Son, to die for us. Children should know that they are important to God.

We also demonstrate to our children that they are important to God and to us by working with them to develop their character. This involves teaching and setting a good example (as we discussed in chapter 3). If you promise to do something, *do it!* Children need to know that they are important enough to you so that when you say something to them, you mean it. And keeping your promises shows that you value the truth.

Another way to demonstrate to children that they are important and to help develop their character is to admit mistakes. Some fathers are so filled with pride that they never admit they are wrong, especially to their kids. Remember that "shortcut" on the family vacation that cost you two extra hours? You should have listened to your wife, but noooooo, you kept driving and then rationalized your mistake. Or how about the time you thought you had communicated clearly, but everyone else heard you say just the opposite? You angrily denounced their testimony and insisted that they all were mistaken. Or do you remember accusing and punishing a child for something someone else had done (maybe even you)? You kept quiet about it figuring that at other times you probably hadn't punished that child for other, unknown infractions.

> Treat the late adolescent like an adult; he's more likely to act like one if he is given the status offered to other adults.
> *James Dobson[2]*

Hey, it's all right to admit that you're wrong and say you're sorry. In fact, when you do, you will be showing that justice and your child are important to you.

Life Notebook

An excellent tool for enhancing communication and building character is a life notebook.

One of the projects that I (Chuck) committed myself to do was to give each son a life notebook when they were six and to complete it when they turned twelve. Before each boy's sixth birthday, I bought a good photo album as a big birthday gift. The album had loose pages held in place by pegs that could be unscrewed. In the front cover, I wrote a paragraph or two about the uniqueness of that child, his importance to me, why I valued him as an individual, something about the special kind of person he would become, and the fact that I loved him very, very much.

The life notebook became Craig's or Brian's from that moment on. Into the book we recorded Bible verses they learned, first and momentous events (for example, first bike, first fish, first camping trip, first ski experience, first day in school—any first that my wife and I could record). And, of course, we included lots of pictures.

Near the front of the book, we categorized each verse of the book of Proverbs, beginning with chapter one and ending with chapter 31. We tried to get through one chapter each time we met for an appointment. We divided the verses into 12 categories such as good and evil, God, son, wisdom, love, pride, and others. The questions that arose during these appointments were worth all the effort. We covered issues that parents don't usually hear about because of the hectic pace of today's families. In Proverbs we discovered how kids become lazy bums, why girls shouldn't get sexually involved with guys, and how to guard the affections of the heart.

My sons valued their life notebooks more than I ever hoped. If you have a strong-willed child, you know what I mean when I say that Myrllis and I didn't have to ask if Craig disliked or liked anything—he always told us exactly how he felt. So when Craig was a senior in high school, I was shocked when he asked what I thought about displaying his life notebook at his graduation open house. After I got up off the floor, I answered that I thought it would be great for his friends to see his Bible verses, grade school pictures, and stick-figure drawings. I could never have dreamed that Craig would place that kind of value on that notebook. By the way, it was the most popular item at the open house. Kids lined up to sit on the couch to thumb through the pages. If he hadn't valued the book, it would not have been on display.

A life notebook is not the only way to communicate biblical values and build character in children, but it is a way that works.

HELP EACH CHILD DEVELOP
A PERSONAL SKILL OR TALENT

As we've discussed earlier, parents are tempted to project their own talents and desires onto their children. So a football-playing father might push his son in sports or an operatic mother might push her daughter in music. In addition, children must contend with the expectations of friends and others in society. Certain talents are valued more than others. For example, the stands are packed for high school basketball or football games, but much fewer people attend cross-country meets. Kids quite naturally will want to participate in the popular activities and the ones that their friends are in. Yet they may get cut from the team or not make the cast of the play. It takes wisdom and sensitivity to accept our children for who they are and not for what we want them to be, and to broaden their perspectives.

Encourage children to explore a variety of options. Whether or not they ever get serious about the sport or other activity, they may discover a hobby, a leisure pastime, or a recreational outlet that can last a lifetime. And some of the childhood activities can be educational. I (Dave) collected just about everything while growing up. I had books of stamps, boxes of rocks and shells, army patches, and baseball cards. I even had an insect collection. Eventually those butterflies, moths, beetles, and other bugs helped me in zoology, biology, and other assorted science classes. I also took piano lessons and sang with my family and in the choir, and I still love music.

Look for your child's strengths, interests, and natural abilities. If he is artistic, encourage him to take art lessons. If she is athletic, encourage her to develop physical skills. Begin working in this area before adolescence, while children are in elementary school. On the other hand, be ready for your child's interests to change as he or she enters adolescence and begins to grow and change.

When my (Dave's) daughters were very young, as was the case with just about all the other girls in the neighborhood, they took dance lessons. I have vivid memories of those dance recitals, when seemingly endless groups of cute, tutu-clad girls walked on stage and moved to the music, with cameras flashing and camcorders whirring. During those early years, Kara and Dana also tried gymnastics for a few seasons. But as they grew taller and their interests changed, they lost interest in ballet and gave up becoming the next Mary Lou Retton. Instead, in junior high they turned to volleyball and other sports. I have often thought about the many dollars spent on dance and gymnastics. But although my daughters didn't continue with those activities, I believe the money was well invested in the girls' self-esteem. They performed well, and Mom and Dad told them so.

Some of the skills, such as team sports, vocal music, art, dance, or writing, are public, with the schools offering classes and opportunities for expression. Others, such as golf, fishing, child care, hunting, computer programming, photography, cooking, and sewing, may be more private and can be developed outdoors or at home. Encourage kids to try a mix of public and private skills. Both can give them a sense of identity.

Developing skills becomes very important during early adolescent years (approximately fifth to eighth grades). Kids in this age group want to feel competent, to be able to do something. That's why junior-highers seem to try out for everything. They are experimenting and trying to learn skills. This provides an excellent opportunity to introduce your son or daughter to a new hobby, sport, instrument, or activity. It's also a good time to teach life skills such as how to be a good friend, how to study, how to communicate with adults, how to get along with the opposite sex, and others. And how about spiritual life skills? Wouldn't it be great if your child learned how to worship, how to pray, how to study the Bible, and how to explain what they believe? They can. You can teach them.

With all this encouragement toward developing new talents and skills, however, we include this warning: children need to know that they are *safe* with us even if they don't achieve, win, or learn in these ventures. That is, if they fail, they should know that we won't put them down for not succeeding. Instead, when the kids come in last or don't get the part, we should affirm them for their effort and redirect their energies into other areas.

AFFIRM EACH CHILD'S GIFTS

In addition to talents and abilities, each child has other positive attributes that need to be affirmed and developed. From very early on, Gail and I (Dave) could see that Kara was very loyal to her friends. So we let her know that we saw that in her and that loyalty and faithfulness were very good qualities to possess. Other positive qualities include kindness, enthusiasm, courage, encouragement, love, sensitivity, leadership, truthfulness, gentleness, discipline, peacemaking, insight, humility, caring, and so forth. Look for those gifts in your children and affirm them.

You might say something like: "I heard what you said to Mark. That was good, and I'm sure Mark feels

Recognize that your children are individuals in their own right, and not carbon copies of yourself. All too often fathers are eager for their children to accomplish that which they themselves have failed to fulfill in their own lives. Yet, their children may have neither the ability nor the interest to follow in that direction. Recognize that they have their own talents and goals which may or may not coincide with yours.

Clyde M. Narramore[3]

better now. That's called encouragement, and I think you have that gift. Good job!" You might also want to show children where those positive attributes are mentioned in Scripture. See especially the Beatitudes from the Sermon on the Mount (Matthew 5:3-12) and the fruit of the Spirit (Galatians 5:22-23).

The Bible also teaches that God gives spiritual gifts to his children. These gifts of the Holy Spirit are mentioned in Romans 12:4-8, 1 Corinthians 12:1-11, and Ephesians 4:11-13. Help older children (12 and up) discover their spiritual gifts; then discuss how they can use their gifts in your church and in other ways.

Affirming the positive attributes in children lets them know that they're special and that they have something to give to others.

DEVELOP A STRONG SENSE OF FAMILY

Although the emphasis of this chapter has been to help you discover and acknowledge each child's uniqueness and individuality, that child should also see how he or she fits into the family—how all the unique individuals in a family work together. Mom, Dad, brother, and sister are not independent people who just happen to eat and sleep in the same house— they are family. The whole is more than the collection of individual parts. Dad, you should take the lead in pulling the family together. You can make it happen. Here are some ideas.

- *Have a spiritual time together* once a week or several times a month. This could take place after a meal or on a Sunday afternoon—any time the family is all together. Make special placemats with specific topics and life issues for discussion. As your kids get older, allow them to lead the discussions. You could also memorize Bible verses during this time. (A great one to use is *The One Year Bible Memory*

Book for Families by Tyndale House.) Hold these family meetings regularly or whenever the time seems right. Be flexible.

- *Establish family rituals and customs.* How do you celebrate birthdays, Thanksgiving, Christmas, Independence Day, and other major holidays? You probably have a lot of fun and food and a regular routine to follow. Add holidays such as Groundhog Day and Columbus Day, and make up your own "days" to celebrate (try Tired of School Day, Last Day of Summer Blowout, Midsummer Night's Scream, etc.). Kids love parties, especially when they are the center of attention.

We've already discussed family traditions and activities in chapter 1 and bedtime rituals in chapter 4. Other rituals can be as simple as Sunday dinner or Dad's barbeque.

And don't forget family vacations. Myrllis and I (Chuck) agreed early in marriage that we would have an annual family vacation, even if it meant buying less furniture in order to pay for it. That was one of our better commitments. We continue to savor the memories of those trips, and our sons comment every now and then about events and unique family experiences that we had long forgotten.

My (Dave's) parents owned a cottage in northern Wisconsin. My memory is packed with great experiences from those weeks of vacation there. Now Gail and I continue the tradition. Each summer we spend at least a week at Lake Nebagamon, and the girls love it.

Finding the right time for a vacation can be tough, and there never seems to be enough money. It takes planning, and that begins with you, Dad. Put it in your schedule!

Building memories is a great way to pull the family together and to acknowledge each person's uniqueness.

- *Discuss your family's history.* Every family has an interesting history with a fascinating cast of characters. To really understand each person's unique identity and contribution to the family, we need to recognize our ancestors and their contributions. Even the skeletons in the family closet are part of the family. And talking about where the family has lived, especially ancestors and older living relatives and ancestors, contributes to the idea of being special and family.

And what does your child's name mean? What special meaning do your family name, your wife's family name, and the grandparents' family names hold? The meaning of one's name can add to that feeling of being unique and special.

- *Hold a family reunion* to help develop a sense of family. Make it small, involving just your parents, siblings, spouses, children, etc., on one side, or make it big and invite every relative you can think of. Either way, there'll be laughter and stories to last a lifetime. Think of the impact when a child meets the person for whom he or she was named, or the insight gained by the child who hears grandma's stories about when Daddy was little. And most kids love to get together with their cousins, whom they rarely see.

Families are collections of diverse and unique individuals with common ancestry and heritage. Children who understand and appreciate their heritage feel special.

To give children the gift of identity, you must acknowledge each one's uniqueness. This involves more than talk; it means action—taking time with each child, treating each one as important, helping develop his or her personal skills and talents, affirming each child's gifts, and developing a sense of family. Children have value to us; they are "somebodies."

"I AM SOMEBODY SPECIAL."

THINK IT THROUGH

1. What special moments can you remember having with your dad when you were young?

2. What favorite family events or traditions did your family have that didn't cost much money?

3. In what ways are you similar to your grandparents? In what ways are your children similar to your parents? (Do they know that?)

4. What skills did your parents help you develop?

5. What traditions will your kids remember from your family? Which ones do you think they will continue with their children?

6. List each child in your family and his or her special skills and abilities.

7. What can you do to help each child discover a special ability or develop a talent?

Check out these related Bible passages:
Psalm 139:14; Acts 10:34-35; Romans 12:4-8; 15:7;
1 Corinthians 12:1-11; Galatians 5:22-23; Ephesians 4:11-13

CHAPTER 9

Appreciate Their Presence

Give Him a Day

What shall I give one small boy?
A glamorous game, a tinseled toy,
A shiny knife, a puzzle pack,
A train that runs on a curvy track?

No, there's plenty of time for such things yet!
Give him a day for his very own,
Just one small boy and his dad alone.
A walk in the woods, a romp in the park,
A fishing trip from dawn till dark.

Give the gift that only you can,
The companionship of his old man.
Games are outgrown, and toys decay,
But he'll never forget if you give him a day.

32-year-old prisoner, Minnesota State Prison

That poem speaks eloquently of a child's need for Dad—
even if it's just for a day. As you have undoubtedly noticed, that

theme runs throughout these pages—the importance of spending time with our kids. And we've seen that our time is a gift that only we can give.

In this book we first discussed the gift of protection (chapters 1–5). Now we are considering the second major gift, the gift of identity (chapters 6–9). At the end of each chapter in this section, we have included a phrase that encapsulates the main idea. Each of these ideas and phrases is important, but they also build on each other—the overlap is intentional. Here are the phrases and their explanations:

- I AM—our children must understand that we know they exist and that we accept them for who they are.
- I AM SOMEBODY—our children also must know that we think they have value and worth.
- I AM SOMEBODY SPECIAL—our kids also need to feel unique and special and that they can do something well on their own.

Now we come to the final statement and last piece of the identity puzzle: I AM SOMEBODY SPECIAL AND GOOD. Beyond acceptance, beyond value, and beyond uniqueness, our children need to know and feel that we *like* them. In other words, we appreciate their presence: we want them around.

When you carve a day out of your busy schedule to spend with a child, you shout that you want to be with him. When you welcome your child as she interrupts your television viewing, newspaper reading, or other important activity, you let her know that she is more important to you than the TV, newspaper, or activity. When you proudly introduce your kids to your friends, through pictures or in person, you proclaim that they are special to you.

Of course it's easy to talk a good game, to say that we like our kids and want to spend time with them. But our actions speak louder than our words.

- A 1985 California study revealed that the average father of preschoolers spends 37 seconds a day actively involved with his children.
- A 1991 public school survey in Maryland showed that parents spend an average of 15 minutes a week in "meaningful dialogue" with their children.
- A recent Gallup Poll commissioned by the National Center for Fathering surveyed more than 3,000 fathers. This poll found that while the majority of those interviewed could identify the traits and actions important for being good fathers, they admitted that they didn't do most of those things.
- Studies show that fathers tend to devote more time to vocation and hobbies than to their role as father.

> Doug Collins has had offers to become an NBA coach or general manager, or a college coach. They may as well stop calling. His life is broadcasting and watching his son Chris, not in that order. "My son has three more years at this [college basketball]. You can't turn the clock back," he said. "If I were coaching and couldn't be here to watch this, I'd be kidding myself. You can't give time back. I need my son in my life very much." And obviously his son needs him.
>
> *Jay Mariotti*[1]

Appreciating our children's presence begins by making time to be with them—both "quantity" and "quality" time as we discussed in chapter 4. But that's just the beginning. We must spend time with each child, doing things that they enjoy.

Spend Time with Each Child

It's important to plan special days, hours, and moments with your children individually. But beyond just taking a child with you or participating together in activities that *you* enjoy, do something that is of interest to the child.

Imagine that you have no interest whatsoever in the game of golf, yet for Christmas your wife gives you a new putter. How would you feel and what would you think? I'm sure you would thank her, but undoubtedly you would wonder what motivated her to buy that gift. *What could she have been thinking?!* Unfortunately, that's how many parents treat their children—taking them to activities and events that are boring at best and calling them "treats" or "special outings."

After a fathering seminar, a man told me (Chuck) about his efforts to find common ground with his 15-year-old daughter. "I've tried a number of things," he said. "One of the latest is to get her to go fishing with me in my $5,000 fishing boat. In fact, I've asked her four times, but she refuses to go. All she wants to do is to go to the mall. And I wouldn't go there on a bet, especially with a teenage daughter!" Obviously this father missed the point that his daughter's enjoyment of the activity is more important than his own.

We should think of how we can spend time with our kids in activities that *they* like. Think of the enjoyment you could bring your little boy or girl by getting down on the floor and playing with the Tonka trucks, Sesame Street puppets, or

> Joey shuffled reluctantly to the blackboard. The teacher had asked him to write one word that best described his dad. The fourth-grader hesitated and then asked, "How do you spell 'selfish'?" He slowly wrote S-E-L-F-I-S-H across the blackboard. The teacher sensed the delicacy of the situation, so she didn't pursue the matter until after class. Then she asked Joey why he chose *selfish*.
>
> "Because he never does anything with me," the boy said meekly. "He's always got time for hunting and fishing by himself and playing golf and playing cards and bowling with his friends. He always does what he wants to do but never what I want to do."
>
> **William Swindell**[2]

Barbie dolls. Older kids would love to have you take them to the amusement park, out for ice cream, to the mall, or to a concert of a favorite music group. That may mean putting up with programs and events that leave you cold, and you may feel as though you are wasting your precious hours and minutes. You may also think you're wasting money on gas or for your admission. There's no doubt that children are expensive.

A group of parents were standing around at a neighborhood party, complaining about their kids and the cost of raising them. A man who had just moved to the neighborhood jumped into the conversation. "I know what you mean," he said. "When my daughter was a baby, we seemed to make countless trips to the store, buying Pampers, baby food, and other supplies. And there were all those visits to the doctor as she was growing up—doctors aren't cheap!

"Then, when she was in grade school, we had all the school supplies to buy. And the lessons—dance, gymnastics, piano—every week I was writing a check to someone!

"But junior high was even worse. My daughter wanted to be in every sport and activity that the school and park district offered. And every time we turned around, the school wanted money for field trips or special events.

"Of course we hadn't seen anything yet. In high school, after my daughter got her driver's license, the insurance premiums went through the roof. And believe me, you don't want to know what prom dresses cost these days!

"But if you really want to talk about spending money. Wait till your kids are in college. Tuition and expenses can run as high as tens of thousands of dollars a year at some schools. We spent all the equity in our house to put our daughter through college."

The man paused for a few seconds, and then he continued: "My daughter died last month. Now she doesn't cost me a dime."

That puts it into perspective. Children are worth it. Yes, it costs in time and money to invest in our children's lives. But consider the alternative . . . could we make a better investment?

PRACTICE WHAT YOU PREACH

Check out the desk of a typical businessman and you will find pictures of his family staring back at you—the wife and kids smiling broadly in the Olan Mills frame. And in his wallet, probably you will find the same—a parade of snapshots of each child from infancy to the most recent school picture. It's also likely that during informal discussions over lunch or at the water cooler, this man will talk about his kids, bragging about their awards and accomplishments.

> I never met a man who said at the end of his career that he wished he had spent more time at work. But I've met many who said they wished they had more pictures of their kids in which they were included.
>
> **Lee Iacocca**

It is true that some fathers don't like their children and are ashamed of them or embarrassed by them. But most dads, especially fathers of infants, toddlers, and grade-schoolers, are proud of their kids and rightfully so. The problem, however, is that often these fathers keep their pride a secret from their kids. In fact, they may act just the opposite. When one boy heard that his father was proud of him he reacted, "If I'm so good, why doesn't he want to be with me?"

Some fathers don't praise their children because they don't want them to have an inflated view of themselves, to become conceited. So these dads suppress their fatherly pride and may even put down their kids at home. Of course it would be foolish to heap excessive praise on our children with statements such as: "You're the prettiest girl in the whole world," "You're the greatest basketball player!" or "That's the best picture I've ever seen." Compliments like those are hard to accept and may, in fact, lead to conceit. But children need to know that their parents like them and appreciate what they've done. Instead of extreme statements like the ones above, we can say something like: "You sure look pretty," "That was an excellent shot you made at the end of the game. You're improving every week!" and "I really like this picture."

Are you proud of your children? Practice what you preach. Spend time with them, and tell them how you feel.

KNOW YOUR CHILD

Before you can offer genuine compliments or spend time in activities that your children enjoy, you have to know them. We make a serious mistake if we assume that they are the same or exactly like us. In chapter 8 we discussed the fact that each child is unique, with his or her own personality, talents, gifts, and dreams. Our children will be like us in many ways, but they are *not* us—they are themselves.

How well do you know your kids? If your child is six years of age or older, can you write down the first names of five of his or her friends? Who are three of his or her heroes? What are your child's favorite subjects in school? What are his or her future goals or aspirations? You can learn about your children through three simple steps: watch, listen, and ask.

> Our children need 100 percent of us. I can't have one eye on the television and one eye on my daughter Sarah's homework. You can't listen to your children when you're still replaying in your mind the big staff meeting at work. Kids have great antennae. They know where they stand in our priorities.
>
> *Gary Bauer[3]*

Watch

This step simply means "Open your eyes!" What pictures adorn the walls of your kids' rooms? What do they like to do with friends? What makes the top 10 on your children's Christmas or birthday lists? Where do they go in the mall?

What magazines and books do they read? Children give all sorts of clues about what they are like and what they enjoy.

My (Dave's) daughters love music: they listen to it on the radio and the stereo, and they sing their favorite songs. A quick perusal of their tape and CD collections would give me a good idea of their musical tastes. And I'm sure I could discover what concerts each one would enjoy attending. One of my daughters is a sports nut—she tries out for every team, enjoys following Chicago's professional sports teams (especially the Bulls), and did a career speech for school on being an athletic trainer. Suppose I got hold of two tickets to a Bulls game. Do you think she'd want to go with me? You bet!

> Everyone says that their dad is the best, but I know in my heart that I've got the best father in the whole world! I want my dad to know how much I love him, because not as often as I'd like to tell him do I say those four meaningful words: I love you, Dad!
>
> **Ninth-grade girl**

Open your eyes and look for the clues to your kids' interests.

Listen

Similar to "watch," this step also means being alert: "Open your ears!" In other words, listen to what your kids talk about. In chapter 5 we discussed the value of learning to listen to our children. Sometimes when we're quiet, we'll be amazed at what our kids will say . . . and what we can learn.

Listen especially for excitement in their voices. What gets them turned on, psyched up, excited? This will give you clues to their interests. Listen at the dinner table, in the car, and especially in conversation.

Ask

Another very effective way to determine your child's interests and aptitudes is to ask. Of course you can go directly to the child with your questions: "If you could do anything this

Saturday, what would you like to do?" "What is your favorite activity?" "If you had $1,000 to spend, what would you buy?"

It will be just as helpful, however, to ask your child's teachers and other adults who regularly interact with him or her. Usually they will be quite willing to share their observations and insights in answer to questions such as these: "In what activities does she show great interest?" "What talents or abilities do you see?" "Where does he have great potential?"

To appreciate our children, we have to know them, and each one is unique. Become a student of each child: watch, listen, and ask.

EXPRESS YOUR LOVE

Kids love to be told that they are appreciated and loved. And *everyone* needs a hug now and then. Verbal and physical expressions of love can be powerful.

Express Love Verbally

How do you talk to your kids? Do your words express how you feel . . . that you love them? Humorous nicknames don't always communicate love and acceptance—often just the opposite; for example, "Twerp," "Dweeb," "Geek," or "Shorty." Instead, we should use positive nicknames that encourage and motivate, such as, "Princess," "Champ," "Sunshine," and "Beautiful" or "Handsome." Many elementary children take on the character of their nicknames.

Some parents rarely use any endearing terms for their child, not even his or her real first name. I (Chuck) got to know a young man who said without a smile, "I was almost nine years old before I knew my name wasn't 'shut-up.'" Label a child with a negative behavior long enough, and, eventually, he or she will act out that behavior.

Remember, you as a father possess great power and influence

over your children. How you address them often will indicate your appreciation of their presence and value.

Greeting our kids by name and with positive comments affirms their self-worth and opens the door to further communication, but there's much more we can say to them. The words "I love you" seem to flow freely to babies and toddlers. But as kids grow older and begin to push the limits and move toward independence, many parents seem to forget that familiar and important phrase. In my work with high school students, I (Dave) have often counseled young people about their relationships with their parents. I am surprised at how many kids say they can't remember the last time their parents, especially their father, told them they loved them. As we discuss this further, most of these students admit that their parents probably love them but just don't know how to express themselves.

There is really only one thing I wish was included in our relationship. I wish he would say that he loves me more often. I know he does through his actions, I mean what kind of a dad would do all this for someone he didn't love? But every night before I go to bed, I say, "Night Dad. Love you. See you in the morning." And he says, "Uh huh." I wish that sometimes he would say I love you back.

Ninth-grade boy

What if your children were asked to recall the last time they were told by their dad, "I love you"? Would they answer immediately, or would they have to think about it for awhile?

Whether because of ethnic heritage, individual personality makeup, or just habit, many families don't express their emotions. That's the way it was in my (Dave's) family—we just didn't verbalize our love for each other very much. Whenever I left my folks' house, whether returning to college as a student or to my home as an adult, I would kiss Mom good-bye and shake Dad's hand. We (all five kids and our parents) didn't hug too often or express our love openly. But about 13 years ago, an incident changed that for me.

Dad had suffered a severe heart attack and had undergone heart bypass surgery. During the time I agonized over his condition and prayed for his recovery, I realized how much I loved him. I lived several states away and had only been with Dad the week before the operation. When I was able to visit again, during the summer, he was still recuperating. Trying to regain the strength in his legs, Dad would walk slowly up and down the street. We would walk together and talk about my kids, sports, his health, the family, and so forth. During each conversation, I would think, *Now's the time for me to say, "I love you."* But I just couldn't do it. Finally it was time to leave again. I kissed Mom good-bye and walked to the car with Dad. Gail and the girls were inside, ready to go. Just before I got in the car, I turned to Dad, gave him a big hug, and whispered, choking back the tears, "I love you, Dad." That may not seem like much, but it was a break-through for me. And from that time on, we had no trouble hugging and saying those magic words. My Dad died a few years ago, and recently I found the last note he wrote me, just two months before his death.

> July 25, 1990
> Dear Dave,
>   HAPPY BIRTHDAY!
>   I love you,
>   Dad

Tell your kids that you love them. It's a gift that money can't buy and that only you can give.

Express Love Physically
We also express our love through touch, a tangible expression of our feelings. Loving touch is especially important . . .

- immediately after discipline, conflicts, and disagreements.
- during periods of grief: after losing a contest, being hurt by a friend, or having a major disappointment.
- during joyous occasions: reaching a goal, winning a victory, receiving an award, overcoming a tough hurdle, or solving a difficult problem.

Don't back off touching your children. Daughters need their fathers to continue to touch them appropriately, even after they have gone through puberty and have developed physically. Of course you should be careful not to embarrass your daughter in public, in front of her friends, but a hug is almost always appropriate. A problem develops when a father treats his daughter differently after she reaches adolescence. Many teenage girls feel rejected when their dads stop touching them after their bodies begin to change.

A Christian college counselor with 18 years of experience said this about college girls who are sexually active. "I think it is safe to say that I have heard most of the struggles that college students face—their search for answers to dysfunctional families and backgrounds, including their desire for acceptance and self-worth. But I wasn't prepared for what I found during the 1989–1990 collegiate year. Twenty of our female students who were sexually active had a common problem. When asked, 'What kind of relationship do you have with your father?' 19 of the 20 had no relationship with their father, and the 20th girl's dad had died when she was 12 years old. The surprise for me was that none of the girls could remember the last time they had been 'touched' appropriately by their fathers."

This points out an incredible need. If girls are not touched appropriately by their fathers, they will likely seek that acceptance and male touch in an inappropriate manner. Even if only temporary, that touch will meet their need to be valued. The girl may not even like the guy, but he provides the feeling of acceptance that she didn't receive (or didn't perceive that she received) from her dad.

Genuine acceptance from Dad is important, not only for the momentary feeling of security it provides, but also because it opens the pathway to healthy relationships in the future. A daughter's first attempts to reach across the sex barrier to please men will be with her own father. She needs to know from him if she is acceptable, if she is attractive, and if her conversation is intelligent. If her dad applauds her mental and spiritual attributes at an early age, she will have the confidence that she doesn't have to rely on shallow sex appeal to attract young men in her growing up years. If her father continues to affirm her in a proper way, she will become convinced that she has importance as a person, not as a sex object.

As this young lady makes worthwhile contributions of her own, her personal confidence will grow and develop. As she learns to please her father, she will be able to handle herself confidently with young men as she matures. Her adult relationships with men will be very positive if triggered by a healthy one with her father.

Keep telling and hugging. Communicate your love verbally and physically.

Your children need to know and believe that you appreciate them and want them around, that you really like just being with them. Then they will know that . . .

"I AM SOMEBODY SPECIAL AND GOOD."

THINK IT THROUGH

1. What special times with your father can you remember from your childhood?

reasonreasonreasonreasonreasonreasonreasonreasonreasonreasonreasonreasonreasonreasonreasonreason

What made those times special?

2. What sacrifices did your parents make to spend time with you as an individual?

3. What family pictures do you have on your desk at work?

4. What can you do to get to know each of your children better?

5. What can you do to demonstrate to your children that you like them?

6. Which child needs to hear you say "I love you"?
When will you say those words to him or her?

7. Which child needs a hug from you?
When will you give him or her that hug?

Check out these related Bible passages:
Psalm 72:4; 127:3-5; Proverbs 17:6; 31:28;
Matthew 19:14-15; Luke 1:17; 2 Corinthians 12:14.

PART THREE

THE *gift* OF CONFIDENCE

Just a few decades ago, divorce was the exception. We knew kids whose parents were divorced, of course, but those families were rare in our experience. Today, however, most American families have felt the pain of marriages torn apart—an aunt, uncle, brother, or sister have been divorced . . . or maybe even Mom and Dad.

Hearing about and seeing the reality of divorce can cause children to feel insecure and afraid. They might ask, "Will you get divorced like Billy's mom and dad?" And learning of a family deserted by a parent will intensify their insecurities.

These fears are real and cannot be allayed simply with words. Talk is hollow when contradicted by hateful and divisive actions. Think about this: What evidence do your children have that you are genuinely committed to the family and to them as individuals?

We can give our kids the gift of confidence. It begins when they know we will stick with them, with their mother, with the family—no matter what! They need this gift, and it's a gift that money can't buy.

CHAPTER 10

Be Consistent

He gives 110 percent every game. He hustles! He plays hurt! I know that I can count on him—that every game he'll suit up and produce for me."

That's how a coach describes a key athlete. What makes the athlete so important to the team and the coach is much more than his ability—it's his dedication and consistency. That athlete leads by his example and inspires confidence in his coach and teammates. His commitment to the team and to winning is not the result of a negotiated contract. In fact, he'd probably play the game for free. The dedicated athlete plays because he loves the game and because he is loyal to his team and his fans.

Consider a contrasting example—the athlete who sits out a game or even a season because he isn't paid enough or appreciated enough. Or the player who seems to find excuses for every poor performance. Teammates soon learn that such an athlete, even one with great ability and skill, cannot be trusted—they can't count on him in the clutch. He seems only to be looking out for himself.

Some people approach marriage as a contract, with the idea that it needs to be negotiated and needs to work for them. Contracts are based on trade-offs; that is, if you give something, you will get something in return. Then, if one side doesn't fulfill the terms of the contract, it can by voided, broken, deserted. Like self-centered athletes, men and women who approach marriage with that attitude get out when the going gets tough.

But God's plan is that marriage is a *covenant,* not a contract. It should be based on commitment, not on performance. It should be permanent—not renegotiated every two or three years. That's why traditional wedding ceremonies include the words "For better or worse, for richer or poorer, in sickness and in health, until death parts us." That's not multiple-choice; it's all or nothing! A spouse may be "worse" and become "poor" and "sick." When we stand at the church altar and intone those solemn vows, we promise lifelong commitment, *no matter what.* Contracts are breakable or renegotiable, but covenants are forever.

A covenant commitment will lead to consistency in marriage, and consistency by parents will build security and confidence in children. Sons and daughters need to know that Mom and Dad will be there, giving 110 percent, playing hurt, always producing for the good of the family team.

CREATE A STABLE LIFE STRUCTURE

One mark of consistency in the family is stability. James says that the unstable, doubtful person is "as unsettled as a wave of the sea that is driven and tossed by the wind" (James 1:6). We want our children to be secure and well, not seasick.

Emotional Strength

Having a stable life structure means being strong emotionally. It means that there is continuity between what is on the inside of the person and how he or she lives on the outside. A stable father, therefore, isn't prone to wide swings of emotion—roaring laughter and then wild anger. Certainly it is right and necessary to show our emotions. The picture of the strong, silent, and emotionless man is a caricature that should be discarded. But we shouldn't swing to the other extreme and be ruled by our circumstances and the emotions they produce in us. Living with an erratic father can be a nightmare. The stable father knows who he is and has his feet firmly planted in reality.

Although my (Dave's) father didn't reveal his emotions and share with his children enough of what he was feeling, one of his strongest attributes was his stability. I never had to worry about my father's emotional state. Even when I needed discipline and knew I would be punished, I never feared that Dad's anger would be out of control

> Is it possible to reconnect fathers to their children? To reverse the societal trends that produced the separation in the first place? To fashion government policies and reshape social attitudes regarding fathers? To change the attitudes of fathers themselves? Probably. But not until we reconvince ourselves of what used to be common sense: Children need their fathers.
> *William Raspberry*[1]

and the punishment extreme. My father also had a wonderful sense of humor—he enjoyed a good joke and loved to laugh. But life wasn't a joke—he knew when to be serious.

Predictability

Having a stable life structure also means that the father is predictable—he doesn't live in either extreme on the continuum separating the "wind" and the "brick wall." The unpredictable "wind" father is changeable, inconsistent, and difficult to understand. The other extreme, the "brick wall" father, is rigid and never changes even though his children change as they mature and develop. Neither of these positions offers the best model for being an effective dad. The brick wall is consistent, but consistently negative.

That was my (Chuck's) experience. Dad was a perfectionist—when I did something with him, it had to be perfect. This made me very insecure and unable, at times, to accomplish the smallest task without the fear of not doing it right. As a young adult, often I would second-guess something that I had done a hundred times. For example, I might measure the same piece of wood three or four times for fear of cutting it wrong. Or I might measure the spot to drill a hole at least three times. You see, I could remember my father being on my case as a boy, especially if I cut the wood wrong or drilled the hole off-center. If I did it right, still I was wrong because I didn't do it *good enough*. Even in my 50s, in the middle of a project, out of nowhere that feeling may emerge—the negative consequences for messing things up. Although I have made tremendous progress over the past several years in dealing with these insecurities, every now and then those feelings appear when I least expect them.

When my boys were quite young, I found that I had a tendency to do the same thing to them as my father had done to me . . . and as his father had done to him. My dad had tried everything to please my grandfather, but he was unsuccessful. In my opinion, that has kept my father from ever having confidence in himself, and he continues to this day to struggle with not being good enough.

Studies indicate that children of inconsistent fathers experience insecurity that carries into adulthood. These adult children live with a sense of fear. Today the world is even more unpredictable than when we were children, so kids carry more anxiety about life and fear about relationships than possibly any time in our nation's history. Newspapers are filled with tragic stories of boys and girls being kidnapped, violence on playgrounds, and handguns in schools. More than ever, children need their homes to be safe, stable, and secure refuges where they belong.

The reality, however, is that many homes are anything but stable. And a home with an unstable, unpredictable, inconsistent father can be devastating to a child because it affects that child's core beliefs about life. As children grow and mature, they develop a basic outlook on life, deciding what is good, right, bad, wrong, and safe, and learning how to trust, how to react and relate, and what the world is like. Think of a child who can never be sure whether his father will hug him or hit him—imagine that child's confusion and fear!

Availability

Being stable and consistent also means being available. We've discussed this in other chapters. Can your children count on you? Do they know when you will be home, that you will be there for them? Many jobs demand that fathers work long hours or travel a lot—they can't drive away from the office at 5:00 every day and walk into the house at 5:30. But even if your circumstances are extreme, you can block out regular time in the schedule for your family and each child. There's no excuse for not communicating when you have to work late, are unexpectedly called away, or travel out of town on business. Being consistent doesn't mean that you have to do everything, every day, at the same time. But it does mean that you are consistently in touch and available.

R**oses are red**
  Violets are blue
I don't know where my dad is,
  Do you?
        Sixth-grade boy

Anticipation

Stability also involves anticipating what might happen in the future. Explaining what to expect in various situations will help children be prepared and bring great comfort to them.

For several years, I (Chuck) have led father-daughter canoe trips into the Boundary Waters Canoe Area in northern Minnesota and father-son trips into Canada. There are several important rules and guidelines for canoeing on large lakes and rivers. I emphasize these rules before the trip because our survival may depend on our ability to anticipate the unexpected in whitewater or in three-foot swells on open water. When paddling against wind-driven water, you can feel as though you will never get to your destination. The same is true with whitewater, except that whitewater is much more relentless and unforgiving. The only way to win the battle is to keep your eyes 20 to 30 yards downstream or, on the lake, to try to read the waves 10 to 20 yards ahead.

An area that I cover during trip orientation is how to handle difficult decisions that may need to be made before one gets to shore. By using reasonable foresight, the father and child may be able to stay dry most of the time.

Canoeing and making wise choices on the river provides a model of family leadership. The person in whitewater who is trying to thread a canoe between boulders knows something that an effective father knows: he can't make critical decisions in a state of panic—there is no room for impulsive thinking. The person who is steering must anticipate what lies ahead as well as deal with what is happening at the moment. Surprises can be disastrous.

Effective fathers have foresight. They are not impulsive or reactionary. By contrast, impulsive fathers often are surprised by situations and events, causing them to act on the spur of the moment. They lose touch with the significance of the circumstances around them; thus, they overreact or underreact in critical situations. Either everything is a crisis, or nothing is a crisis. They appear uncertain in their choices. Impulse-directed fathers are always on the edge.

Be the model of stability for your kids. Let them know that they can depend on you.

BE TRUTHFUL

Another mark of consistency is truthfulness. We need to be committed to the truth, men who will keep our word. Our children should know that they can believe us. If they can believe us, then they can have confidence in us. This will encourage them to be truthful as well and to have confidence in themselves.

Being truthful begins as a personal conviction. It is a standard of conduct that a family decides to maintain because Mom and Dad have made it a priority. Other convictions and standards will differ from family to family, even among Christians. But lying should not be an option if we want to develop character and confidence in our kids.

Unfortunately, truthfulness has fallen by the wayside along with other traditional values in our society. Many recent polls have indicated that most Americans will do or say almost anything if it helps them get ahead. Today we wonder if there's anyone we can trust. No wonder people are losing confidence in government, in the school system, in business leaders, and in themselves.

God's Word is clear—we are to speak the truth (Proverbs 23:23), love the truth (John 18:37), be committed to the truth (Ephesians 4:25), be focused on the truth (Philippians 4:8), and rejoice in the truth (1 Corinthians 13:6). In fact, lies are from Satan, the father of lies (John 8:44). Anything less than the truth is sin.

Truthfulness is a foundation block for building a solid family. Respect for truth should be established with each child when he or she is very young. Make it very plain that lying will be met with the severest of punishments. Truthfulness, on the other hand, will be enthusiastically affirmed.

Making truthfulness a priority in the home begins with the parents. Remember, your children will pick up the values you model (see chapter 3). If you really want your children to believe you and to believe *in* you, say what you mean and mean what you say. Don't threaten discipline that you won't follow through with. And when you are wrong, own up to your mistake or sin; don't make excuses or try to cover it up. Improper behavior that is covered up by lying should be the ultimate crime in your home, for *you* as well as the kids.

> I like the way you tell me the truth about everything. When I grow up and have kids, I want to be just like you.
>
> *From a letter to a father from his son; quoted by Ann Landers*[2]

On the other hand, work hard at affirming and rewarding children for telling the truth, even when it is painful for them to do so.

This basic family rule really paid off when my (Chuck's) oldest son was six. We lived in Muskegon, Michigan, at the time. One day, someone set a fire in a vacant lot, and the fire department had to be called to put it out. Almost as soon as the fire fighters began to douse the flames, the police arrived on the scene and started asking questions. One of the kids in the neighborhood had seen my son with a box of matches earlier in the day. It didn't take the police very long to decide that Craig was the culprit.

I took my son aside and asked him just one question: "Craig, did you start the fire?" He answered: "Dad, I had nothing to do with it."

That's all I needed. I informed the police officer that I truly believed my son had not started the fire. The officer asked about my reasons for reaching that conclusion and why I felt

Craig was telling the truth. When I explained, he accepted my answers and then began to question other kids. Later the same day, another boy confessed to having set the fire. That day Craig learned a lifelong lesson—the importance of having a history of telling the truth. Because Craig had established a pattern of consistently telling the truth, I knew I could trust his word.

So the question is: Can your children trust your word? Have you established a pattern of consistently telling the truth?

Being truthful begins with what we tell our kids. Think of how you respond to your son or daughter's questions. Do you gloss over your mistakes and never admit to being wrong? That's not being truthful. Do you promise your kids anything, just to get them off your back? That's not being truthful. Do you make up stories when you don't want kids to have certain information? That's not being truthful. Of course, children don't have the right to know everything we do, and sometimes certain information may be harmful to them. In those cases, just tell them that you can't reveal that information or explain that situation right then, and why. It's easy to skirt the truth or to tell a lie, but that destroys trust.

Being truthful also involves what our children hear us say to others. When someone calls and you don't want to talk to him, do you instruct your daughter, "Tell him I'm not home"? That's a lie. Do you make excuses to your son's teacher about his poor performance in school? That's a lie. Do you promise to do something, never intending to carry it out? That's a lie. If you are inconsistent in telling the truth, don't be surprised if your children become liars.

This gift of truthfulness is one of the most long-lasting gifts you can give your kids. It will influence every area of their lives for as long as they live. But they won't become truthful suddenly or by magic—they have to see it in your life and hear it from your lips. Your consistent commitment to being truthful is the only way.

BUILD HOPE

Remember anticipating that long-awaited family vacation? As the departure date drew near, you became so excited you could hardly stand it. The vacation trip seemed to consume all your thoughts and energy (and you probably drove your parents crazy). You lived each moment in reference to that trip. A future event, something to look forward to, can give us hope and add meaning to our lives in the present.

On a grand scale, this is a profound truth of the Christian life. The apostle Paul wrote of our "blessed hope—the glorious appearing of our great God and Savior, Jesus Christ" (Titus 2:13, NIV). Because we have hope in the future, we can live confidently today, no matter what we're going through. (See also 1 Peter 1:3 and 1 John 3:1-3.)

> Teenagers who had serious delinquency records or mental or emotional health problems were far more likely to straighten out as adults if they lived in a two-parent family, according to a new study.
>
> *Pioneer Press*[3]

Now, bringing it back to your family life and your children, think of what gives them hope—what do they see in their future? You can provide that hope.

Treat Your Kids with the Future in Mind

This simply means to get into the habit of envisioning the kind of man or woman that you want your boy or girl to become. Then consider what you can build into your child's life *now* that he or she will need in the future. Or, on the negative side, think of the midcourse corrections that you may have to make.

I (Dave) have been actively involved in a ministry to junior high young people. Although the patterns for their lives are not set in cement, I certainly can see the directions that many of them are headed. Sometimes I'm wrong, but too often my predictions turn out to be correct. And I'm not just talking about non-Christian families. I have seen the seeds of bitterness, rebellion, and self-centeredness put down roots and emerge later as kids move through high school. At times I feel like screaming at parents, "Don't you see what's happening here? Can't you see the path your child is taking?" I want them to step in and change the course.

Children and young people tend to focus only on the present or the near future. To a very young child, a year seems like an eternity, as does a decade to an adolescent. So we shouldn't be surprised when they are shortsighted or fail to plan. But we're different. As adults, we have a broader perspective—we understand that time passes quickly and that present decisions can have a powerful future impact. So we must work at helping our sons and daughters see that we and God love them for who they are and that we also are interested in who they are becoming. We must say no to activities and habits that will harm them. We also must en-

> I spend all the time I can with my dad 'cause he is usually on the phone or out of town. He has worked at his company for 17 years and is going to retire at the age 55. In his spare time he'll watch TV or work on the computer. The weird thing about him is that he will take a nap at 10:30 P.M. because he is tired and old he says. I tell him to go to bed. He says, "No way." Well, that's my dad's life!!!
>
> *First-grade boy*

courage them in activities and habits that will help them mature, grow, and prepare for the future. These include discovering and developing talents, learning skills, exercising personal discipline, using time wisely, and applying God's Word. We must consistently insist that they do what is right and good for them, even if that is tough for them to take.

Along these lines, it will help to look back with your son or daughter and talk about how he or she has grown and changed over the years. Get out the baby book—look at the family photo album. Then together look forward and talk about the ways in which your son or daughter hopes to grow and change in the future. This also may give you the opportunity to share your own growth experiences—lessons you have learned along life's way. Remember, the future begins now.

Be a Good Example of What It Means to Be an Adult

Many children don't want to grow up because the adult world seems too scary and sad. What image do your children have of being a parent? a homeowner? a husband? a church member? If they hear you only complain about each of those areas, they certainly won't look forward to becoming any of them. It's not that we should hide all our feelings and our problems and pretend that everything is wonderful. But we should make sure not to do the opposite.

Take fathering, for example. It can be a pain. Just thinking of all the investment of time, money, and emotions in your children is enough to trigger deep depression! But balance that picture with the pleasures and joys—her first step, his first word, the tiny outstretched arms running to greet you as you enter the house, his home run, her solo, his first date, the recital, the big game . . . and the thrill of leading them to Christ. Some parents seem to spend all their time complaining about the problems of parenting and telling the kids what a pain they are. If you were a child and that's all you heard, would you want to grow up and become a mom or dad? Probably not. Take time to tell your kids about the joys of parenting and how much you love being *their* father. Remember, being a parent is costly, painful, and tiring, but it's the most important and most rewarding job in the world.

Your consistent commitment to being a good dad, loving your kids, and spending time with them, will spark their desire to repeat the process and one day be good parents too. That gives them hope for the future and builds their confidence in the present.

Be consistent with your family by creating a stable life structure, being truthful, and building hope. That will give your children the gift of confidence, a gift that money can't buy. Let them know that . . .

"DAD IS HERE."

THINK IT THROUGH

1. What's the difference between a contract and a covenant?
   Was your parents' marriage more like a contract or a covenant?
   How do you know?

2. What can you remember about your father's daily schedule?

3. Was your father more like the "wind" or a "brick wall"?
   Where are you on the continuum between those extremes?

4. What can you do to let your kids know how to get in touch with you at all times?

5. At what times is it difficult for you to be a truthful person?

6. What can you do to build hope in your children?

7. What picture of parenthood do your children have from observing you?

8. What do you really enjoy about being a dad?
   How can you share that joy with your kids?

   Check out these related Bible passages:
   Proverbs 5:18; 23:23; John 8:44; 18:37; 1 Corinthians 13:6;
   Ephesians 4:25; Philippians 4:8; Titus 2:12-13; 1 Peter 1:3;
   1 John 3:1-3.

CHAPTER 11

Be Relaxed

I'M supposed to write this about my dad because my English teacher has assigned this to us. I don't really want to because a couple of years ago I stopped communicating with mine. Yeah, sure, I still talk to him and all, but not as a friend, more as a stranger. My father used to be happy, caring, kind, and considerate. Now he's extremely depressed, sad, grumpy; but I know he still loves us. He doesn't express that to any of us: my two brothers or even my mother.

Eighth-grade student

Many modern fathers mirror that image. Carrying the weight of the world, they withdraw emotionally from their families and become quiet, uptight, "grumpy." They pull back and pull away, just when children most need love and nurture from both parents. Traditionally men score lowest in comforting, encouraging, affirming, and listening. As we have already discussed, many teenagers and young adults cannot remember when they heard

Dad say, "I love you." Instead, mothers tend to be the nurturers, while fathers remain the strong, silent providers.

But children need emotional support from Dad too. Instead of being uptight, guarded, and closed, we fathers should be relaxed, vulnerable, and open, taking the initiative in offering affirmation and comfort.

Healthy families deal realistically with life, admitting problems and struggles, and working together to meet each challenge. In healthy families, both Mom and Dad lead, discipline, comfort, and nurture. Healthy families develop problem-solving techniques to meet crises. Family members admit that they don't have all the answers, and they work as a unit to find the answers they need. Members of healthy families have hope for solving problems and resolving crises because family members are free to thoroughly discuss the issues, to air their feelings openly. Family members can say how they feel without being put down; they can be open about their struggles; they can be themselves.

> Most of the dads I talk with have little or no input or feedback on their fathering skills. Even more surprising is the number of fathers who want to improve their fathering skills but don't know how!
>
> **Chuck Aycock**

By contrast, an unhealthy family environment is characterized by little or no freedom and very little positive interaction. Although unhealthy families can maintain the appearance of being functional by denying that problems exist (family members may even believe that their environment is normal), eventually family members pay the price. These are the characteristics, the unwritten rules, of unhealthy families:

1. Don't feel. Family members deny their feelings because those feelings are not affirmed or accepted as valid by others in the family, especially the parents, or because the unspoken rule is that no one is to have bad or contrary feelings.

2. *Don't talk.* Family members, especially children, learn to keep their thoughts and feelings inside for fear of being ridiculed, threatened, or punished. A fifth-grade girl expressed the situation this way: "If I express how I feel, I know my dad will get really mad. The last time I told him how I felt, he said I was ungrateful and didn't appreciate all the things he does for me." According to a sixth-grade boy, "When my friends ask me about our family, what it's like at our house, I can't say because my dad won't let me tell anybody what happens in our home, good or bad."

3. *Don't trust.* Parents teach children not to trust anyone (including them). This breeds fear and anxiety, and it builds a family lifestyle where instability, uncertainty, and insecurity are the norm.

4. *Don't rock the boat.* Children get the message that their opinions are wrong and have no worth. They are not to question the parents' decisions or the family's lifestyle. One father expressed his frustration at this family atmosphere: "We have been married for 13 years. My mother thinks my family should operate like she and my dad functioned. I observed her trying to manipulate my wife, to arrange our kitchen the way my mother thought it should be. When I spoke the truth about what I saw, I became the bad guy. It came down to the fact that if I didn't let her arrange the kitchen that way, I would be destroying our family tradition."

Of course no family is perfect—completely functional or entirely dysfunctional. Rather, all families have elements of both and can be placed on a scale somewhere between highly functional and highly dysfunctional. But fathers can be the catalysts for helping families function better. This gift will help children gain confidence in themselves and in the future. And it's a gift that money can't buy.

BE OPEN

The first step that we dads can take toward building emotionally healthy families is to be open about our feelings, what we're going through. The classic picture of the macho male is the man who is strong and silent, keeping his feelings inside, especially sorrow and fear—he's always in control, always in charge. In reality, that man may be churning internally, devastated by a loss but afraid to cry, or paralyzed by insecurity or fear but afraid to ask for help. He's supposed to be John Wayne, Clint Eastwood, and Arnold Schwarzenegger. Then, unfortunately, he passes on that attitude to his children. "Don't be a crybaby!" he yells with each child's whimper or sign of a tear.

I (Dave) can remember thinking that my father never had any problems (except with us kids) because he seldom shared his worries or fears with anyone except Mom. I know he meant well—he didn't want to worry us or to make us afraid of the future. But a little more vulnerability would have been helpful. In the last few years of his life, we had a wonderful time talking, crying, laughing, and praying together.

> **If I could go back and change some things in my life that dealt with my father, I would say we needed more quality time. We needed to open up to each other more. I should have openly tried to talk with him about his drinking. Maybe he would have drank less.**
>
> ***Twelfth-grade student***

Men, it's all right to cry; it's all right to admit weaknesses; it's all right to ask for help.

We fathers need to be good role models of how to deal with our feelings by allowing our children to see us struggle with the gritty issues of life. We can show our kids how to deal with emotions in a healthy, positive way and how to disagree and not keep feelings bottled up inside. This involves owning our feelings, whether it's anger toward the wife or disappointment with the behavior of a child or someone else. For example, when you and your wife have an argument over letting your daughter go down the street to play just before dinner, you can let your child know that you are angry with her mother and that it has nothing to do with her. (Children often think that they have caused the fight or problem.) Then let your daughter know how you resolved the issue.

Being open also means being honest. In chapter 3, we discussed the importance of modeling integrity, and in chapter 10, we emphasized being truthful. In addition, we should be honest with ourselves and our kids. Some fathers think that healthy families don't have problems, and that if they have struggles they shouldn't admit it because doing so would be a sign of weakness. These fathers try to keep up the happy family image in the neighborhood and at church. In reality, healthy families have struggles; they just have a different way of looking at them and dealing with them. Healthy families expect problems and consider them to be a normal part of life. And they work together to find solutions. In fact, the first step to solving any problem is acknowledging that the problem exists.

It's not that we should parade our dirty laundry for all the neighbors to see. But our friends and neighbors should know that we struggle and hurt too, and that our kids are not perfect, just like theirs. The need to look good at any cost will force us to keep secrets that can cripple our children emotionally, causing them to be dependent on an unhealthy family system, rather than moving toward independence.

Of course, part of being honest is admitting when we've made a mistake, when we're wrong, and when we don't have all the answers. That's been a real struggle for me (Chuck), and

I've found it to be a common problem with many men I've talked to. We men seem to have an enormous fear of appearing to have failed and of admitting that we don't know something.

By admitting our mistakes and failures to our children, we free them to be less than perfect. By admitting our problems and looking for help, we free our children to do the same. Earlier in this book I (Chuck) shared about my struggle growing up and how I was destined to repeat the unhealthy father-child relationship with my boys. With little or no father modeling, I had no idea what a healthy father did or how he related to his children. The truth is that unless I had gotten help in developing healthy fathering patterns, my sons probably would have grown up perceiving life in extremes, judging themselves mercilessly, struggling in intimate relationships, and being susceptible to substance abuse and other extreme behaviors.

I'm very grateful to God that I did get help and that my children were spared having an uninvolved father. It was imperative for me to have feedback on my fathering. That all began by admitting to myself that I had a problem and that I needed help.

By admitting to having problems and then seeking help for them, you can free your children to be all that God designed them to be. It also will break the cycle of dysfunction for your grandchildren.

Give your kids the gift of openness and honesty. This gift will enable them to become emotionally healthy young men and women, with the confidence and independence to grow healthy families themselves.

CHILL OUT
The second step we dads can take to build emotionally healthy families is to keep our cool, even when things get hot.

This means controlling our temper and carefully choosing our battles. One way to figure out whether an issue is worth a fight is to ask ourselves, "Will this matter in three to five years?" Some dads go crazy over the slightest infraction or slip by a child.

Actually, many of the actions of children are simply a result of them being young—they are just acting their age. For example, suppose you asked your sixth-grade daughter to clear the table after dinner. Reluctantly she picks up the dishes, rinses them off, and puts them in the dishwasher. You leave the table, thinking that the job will be done right. When you return, however, you find a few dishes still on the table and a couple next to the sink. How do you think you would react? Many parents would chew the girl out. It's quite possible, however, that she got distracted or honestly didn't realize she wasn't finished. Remember, this is an early adolescent with a very short attention span. Is this an issue worth fighting about? Not really. A better response would be to call your daughter back in the kitchen and calmly explain to her what else she needs to do to finish the job.

Other preteen and teenage situations that seem to drive parents crazy include use of the phone, care of personal belongings, mess-leaving, and tastes in music and clothes. We need to remember that the issues worth fighting over are those that

> I talked too much. I had good material, but I used it indiscriminately. I used the same two-hour speech on filling their glass too full of milk as I used when they stayed out all night without calling home. The speech lost its effectiveness.
> *Erma Bombeck*[1]

will affect our children's character and impact their future. It's possible to win a battle and lose the child. Don't get hot; keep your cool.

"Chilling out" also means being able to laugh at ourselves. Some fathers are stiff and uptight, afraid to break image, much like a high school student trying to maintain his cool in front of his peers. Freddie Langston, a great communicator to youth through music, often leads thousands of teenagers in singing. Knowing that some kids are afraid to let go of their image and let their hair down and perhaps appear childish, he challenges them, "Don't be too cool to be a fool!" His point is that if they stand back as "cool" observers and not get involved, they will miss out on all the fun.

Our kids need to see us be vulnerable, take chances, get involved. This will help them relax and be themselves. And it will give them a positive image of adulthood—they will see that growing up doesn't mean always being serious and uptight.

It's great watching church elders work in the nursery, a CEO get a pie in the face in a skit, a tough truck driver share his testimony, a lawyer act in a Sunday school drama, and a variety of dads participate in crazy games at the church picnic. Don't take yourself so seriously—laugh at yourself, chill out, get real, relax.

HAVE FUN

A few years ago, the refrain to a popular song exclaimed that "girls just want to have fun!" That's true about little girls and boys as well as their older sisters and brothers. And children want their dads to have fun too!

Fathers who can laugh with their kids become real to them and not merely authority figures, disciplinarians, or stiff caricatures of other roles they must assume. Although my (Dave's) dad was an imposing figure at six feet three and 235 pounds and a strong enforcer of the rules around the house, I never felt overwhelmed or threatened by him. One reason, of course, is because I knew that Dad loved me and would do anything for me. But I also could relax with him because he always had a twinkle in his eye. Dad enjoyed telling and hearing jokes—he loved to laugh. When I was very young, my father sang in the Lorimer Quartet, out of the Lorimer Baptist Church in Chicago. In addition to singing in church services, these men would perform at banquets and other social events. That's where I first saw Dad in some crazy skits. I also saw him goof around in choir and make creative and humorous trophies to present to choir members at their annual dinner. We also had fun together—we would shoot baskets or play catch, and we enjoyed trips to Wrigley Field or Milwaukee County Stadium and terrific family vacations. Dad was fun, and he was real.

Having fun with our children means relaxing and not taking their small mistakes and life itself so seriously. It means leaving work at the office. It involves taking time, loosening the tie, rolling up the sleeves, and getting down to their level.

When children are very young, we can tickle, play hide-and-seek, tag, and ring-around-the-rosy. With older children, we can play board games, card games, Ping-Pong, pool, basketball, baseball, and many other fun activities. Teenagers want to have fun too, and we can enjoy life with them. We can play Sticky Situations (Tyndale House Publishers) or the Ungame, rent a funny video, listen to a comedy tape, play golf or tennis, and go to a professional or college sporting event or theatrical performance.

We should look for ways to laugh and enjoy life together. And, by the way, we should always remember the purpose for the games we play—to have fun together, not to win. Many fathers remember the day when their sons beat them for the first time in one-on-one basketball, tennis, Ping-Pong, or golf—it was a humbling experience. But some fathers are not good losers, and some even cheat at the games. In that case, it would be better not to play. Play hard; play fair; have fun; and win or lose gracefully.

157

Another way to have fun together as a family is to tell jokes. If you don't have a quick wit or have trouble remembering humorous anecdotes, buy a joke book. Work at developing a sense of humor. It's great to be able to laugh with each other.

Good parents want to build confident and emotionally healthy kids. You can help do just that, Dad, by being open, chilling out, and having fun. Relax and let your kids know that . . .

"DAD IS REAL."

THINK IT THROUGH

1. What do you think was your father's biggest problem when he was 25 years old? 35? 45?

2. In what ways did you help your father with his problems?

3. When you were growing up, what did your family do for fun?

4. In what ways did your father display his sense of humor?

5. Would your children describe you as closed or open? tense or relaxed? serious or fun?

6. What can you do to be more open with your family?

7. What can you do to have more fun at home?

Check out these related Bible passages:
Deuteronomy 12:7; Psalm 126:2-3; Proverbs 12:25; 15:13, 15; 17:22; Ecclesiastes 4:8-12; Matthew 6:25-34; Galatians 6:2.

CONCLUSION

It's gift-giving season again. Whether for Christmas, birthdays, Easter, graduation, or another special occasion, it seems as though Dad is always paying for presents for at least one of the kids. Although the process is painful for a few minutes as Dad writes the check, he soon realizes that the smiles, squeals of delight, and "thanks, Dad" of his son or daughter are worth any amount of money. Good fathers enjoy giving gifts to their children and are always seeking gifts that are just right and "just what I always wanted."

In reality, the most important gifts cannot be found in malls and come with no financial price tag attached. They are priceless gifts that money can't buy. Yet, these are gifts every father can give . . . and they are gifts that every child needs.

It's not that these gifts are free—there is a cost to be paid in time, energy, and attention. Dad must purchase these gifts for his children, one child at a time and one day at a time—the gift of PROTECTION, the gift of IDENTITY, and the gift of CONFIDENCE.

Over the previous pages we've discussed those gifts in great detail and have explained what you can do to give them to your children. The call of this book has been to create a gift-giving climate in your family. We pray that you will take our words to heart and determine to be a gift-giving dad.

A few years ago, the world lost Gerald "Rink" Ringenberg to leukemia. Rink was a Midwest farmer, a strong Christian, and a dedicated father. At his death, his son, Brent, wrote a poem about his dad. Between the lines, you can read the legacy left from father to son.

Big Shoes

In the eyes of a little boy,
A Dad wears big, big shoes.

I remember your big shoes, Dad.
I remember . . .

> *Big shoes that meant business!*
> *Big work shoes*
>   *lined up along the basement wall*
> *Shoes for every farm occasion*
>   *High shoes, low shoes, chasing-after-pigs shoes*
>   *Chores shoes, tractor shoes, going-to-town-for-lunch shoes*
>   *Leather shoes, rubber shoes, always-on-the-go shoes*
> *Shoes that knew where they were going!*
>   *Big shoes, busy shoes, helping-out-the-neighbor shoes*
>   *Working long hours dawn-to-dusk-and-beyond shoes*
>   *Tie shoes, buckle shoes, shoes with corn, straw, oats,*
>   *hay, beans inside*
> *Shoes that knew a little animal "psychology"*
>   *child psychology too*
> *These were the big work shoes of my Dad,*
>   *a happy whistler, a man*
>   *who loved his work*
>   *who worked with love*
>   *in his heart.*

I remember, Dad . . .

> *Big shoes that loved to play—*
>   *Sports shoes, games shoes, happy-just-for-fun shoes*
>   *Ping-Pong, pool, golf, and tennis shoes*
>   *A big shoe on your croquet ball*
>   *sending mine out of sight*

A big shoe on bicycle pedals
    sporting a little boy on the handlebars
        all around town
Quick shoes (spikes!) getting (or getting out of the way of)
    hot smashes at third
High top black tennies
    pivoting, leaping, shooting, swishing!
Cleated shoes that loved to roam the country
    searching not errant pigs
        but little white dimpled balls
Slippers under the old oak kitchen table
    removed to concentrate on the next move
        Uno, Rook, Scrabble, Wahoo!
Busy shoes that stopped at the slightest coaxing
    to play ball with a kid
    or travel hours
        to watch him ride the bench
    or visit a friend
        or older relative in need
With his easy laugh and quick wit
    gracious in victory and defeat,
    these were the playing shoes of my Dad,
        a big, big winner!

I remember, Dad . . .

Saturday nights
    Bath and shoe-polishing night
    Wingtips and dress loafers
        lined, shining, big and little
            along the antique bathroom chest
    These were the very special Sunday shoes
        of "Farmer Bill," a man equally at home
            in church or barnyard

These were the serious shoes of competitor "Rink"
    who found in any ball field his mission field
These were the glistening dress-up shoes of my Dad,
    a quiet, distinctly Christian man
    whose love and deep spiritual devotion
    continue to inspire us all.

And now, Dad, as you put on
    shoes of greater rest and recuperation
    we see clearly their true size
    and your true character
    and we know deep in our hearts, that
No one can fill them but you.

Yes, I remember . . .

    To a little boy
    A Dad wears big, big shoes.

Brent Ringenberg
27 November 1988

What legacy will you leave? What gifts will you give?
From Dad, with love!

162

NOTES

INTRODUCTION

1. Tom Hamburger, *Minneapolis Star Tribune,* 10 May 1992. (Hamburger is the Washington Bureau Correspondent for the *Star Tribune.*)
2. Don Eberly, from an interview in *Citizen* magazine, 21 December 1992. (Eberly was formerly the Deputy Director of Public Liaison in the Reagan Administration.)
3. Roger Thompson, *Vision Chattanooga,* Winter 1992.
4. Festus Obiakor, *Vision Chattanooga,* Winter 1992.
5. Samuel Osherson, *Finding Our Fathers* (New York: The Free Press, 1986), 29.

CHAPTER 1: PROVIDE COMFORT

1. Danae Dobson, "Memories of a Great Childhood," in *What My Parents Did Right,* ed. Gloria Gaither (Nashville, Tenn.: Star Song, 1991), 75.
2. Greg Johnson and Mike Yorkey, *Daddy's Home* (Wheaton, Ill.: Tyndale House, 1992), 54.
3. Gordon MacDonald, *The Effective Father* (Wheaton, Ill.: Tyndale House, 1977), 60.

CHAPTER 2: SET BOUNDARIES

1. Joe Klein, "Whose Values," *Newsweek,* 8 June 1992.
2. Roger Freeman of Stanford University; quoted by U.S. Senator Dan Coates in "America's Youth: A Crisis of Character," *Imprimis* (monthly journal of Hillsdale College).
3. *New York Times,* 9 June 1990.
4. Ibid.
5. James Dobson, *The New Dare to Discipline* (Wheaton, Ill.: Tyndale House, 1992), 6.
6. Ibid., 7.
7. Clyde M. Narramore, *Psychology for Living,* June 1992.
8. Pat Gardner, "Growing Pains," *Minneapolis Star Tribune;* summarized from Mary Ann Little and Kevin Karlson, *Loving Your Children Better* (Westport Publishers, 1991).

CHAPTER 3: MODEL VALUES

1. Joe Klein, "Whose Values," *Newsweek,* 8 June 1992.
2. *American Family Association Journal,* November/December 1991.
3. Quoted in ibid.
4. *Time,* May 1991.
5. Lawrence J. Crabb, Jr., "Relationship: Nothing Matters More," in *What My Parents Did Right,* ed. Gloria Gaither (Nashville, Tenn.: Star Song, 1991), 53.
6. David Blankenhorn, "Father Who Stays with Family Bucks Major New Trend," *Minneapolis Star Tribune,* Tues., August 1992, Commentary. (Blankenhorn is president of Institute for American Values.)
7. Courtney Baldwin, "Forgiving Mom," *Campus Life,* February 1993, 50.
8. Russell Kirk; quoted by U.S. Senator Dan Coats, "America's Youth: A Crisis of Character," *Imprimis* (monthly journal of Hillsdale College).
9. C. S. Lewis, *The Abolition of Man* (New York: Macmillan, 1947), 35.
10. Dan Coates, "America's Youth: A Crisis of Character."
11. MacDonald, *The Effective Father,* 108.
12. Clyde M. Narramore, *Psychology for Living,* June 1992.

CHAPTER 4: BE AVAILABLE

1. Christopher N. Bacorn, "Dear Dads: Save Your Sons," *Newsweek,* 7 December 1992. (Bacorn is a psychologist from Boerne, Texas.)
2. Joe Klein, "Whose Values," *Newsweek,* 8 June 1992, 19.
3. Ibid., 21
4. McLanahan and Booth, 1989.
5. MacDonald, *The Effective Father,* 84.
6. Bacorn, "Dear Dads: Save Your Sons," 13.

CHAPTER 5: LISTEN WITH UNDERSTANDING

1. Paul Tournier, *To Understand Each Other* (Richmond, Va.: John Knox Press, 1967).
2. From a letter to a father from his son; quoted by Ann Landers, *Minneapolis Star Tribune,* 16 June 1991.

CHAPTER 6: ACCEPT UNCONDITIONALLY

1. Darryl Savage, *Minneapolis Star Tribune,* 14 January 1993. (Savage was a reporter for WCCO-TV in Minneapolis, Minnesota, and a positive force in the black community.)

2. *New York Times,* March 1991.
3. Margo Maine, *Father Hunger* (Gurze Books, 1991).
4. Patty Carney-Bradley, from her seminar, "Fathering Successful Daughters"; quoted in *Life Balance,* October/November 1992.

CHAPTER 7: AFFIRM WORTH
1. David Blankenhorn, *Washington Post,* May 1992.
2. William Swindell, *Fathers, Come Home* (South Bend, Ind.: Greenlawn Press, 1993), 80.
3. Danae Dobson, "Memories of a Great Childhood," 74.

CHAPTER 8: ACKNOWLEDGE UNIQUENESS
1. R. David Thomas, *Dave's Way* (New York: Berkley Books, 1992), 104.
2. James Dobson, *Dare to Discipline* (Wheaton, Ill.: Tyndale House, 1970), 101.
3. Clyde M. Narramore, "A Personal Word," *Psychology for Living,* June 1992, 2.

CHAPTER 9: APPRECIATE THEIR PRESENCE
1. Jay Mariotti, "Chris Collins, a Senior in Duke Pressure Cooker," *Chicago Sun-Times,* 19 March 1993, Sports.
2. William Swindell, *Fathers, Come Home,* 80-81.
3. Gary Bauer, *Our Journey Home* (Waco, Tex.: Word, 1992).

CHAPTER 10: BE CONSISTENT
1. William Raspberry, *Chicago Tribune,* 17 May 1993, Section 1.
2. Dear Ann Landers, *Minneapolis Star Tribune,* 16 June 1991.
3. Emmy Werner, *St. Paul Pioneer Press,* 18 April 1990.

CHAPTER 11: BE RELAXED
1. Erma Bombeck, At Wit's End, "Quiz for Parents Asks Tough Questions,"(Field Enterprises, Inc., 1984).

Additional titles from Dave Veerman

GETTING YOUR HUSBAND TO TALK *(New! Spring 1994)*
With Gail Veerman 0-8423-1325-7
100+ ideas to get conversations going with your husband.

GETTING YOUR KID TO TALK *(New! Spring 1994)*
0-8423-1326-5
100+ ideas to get conversations going with your children.

HOW TO APPLY THE BIBLE
0-8423-1384-2
Proven techniques for applying God's Word—based on the *Life Application Bible*.

THE ONE YEAR BIBLE MEMORY BOOK FOR FAMILIES
0-8423-1387-7
Daily verses, review questions, and notes help families memorize and understand Scripture.